A Ragged Mountain Press
WOMAN'S GUIDE

GOLF

A Ragged Mountain Press
WOMAN'S GUIDE

GOLF

SUSAN COMOLLI DAVIS

Series Editor, Molly Mulhern Gross

RAGGED MOUNTAIN PRESS / McGRAW-HILL
Camden, Maine • New York • Chicago • San Francisco
Lisbon • London • Madrid • Mexico City • Milan • New Delhi
San Juan • Seoul • Singapore • Sydney • Toronto

Look for these other Ragged Mountain Press Woman's Guides

Backpacking, Adrienne Hall
Canoeing, Laurie Gullion
Climbing, Shelley Presson
Fly Fishing, Dana Rikimaru
Mountaineering, Andrea Gabbard
Powerboating, Sandy Lindsey

Sailing, Doris Colgate
Scuba Diving, Claire Walter
Sea Kayaking, Shelley Johnson
Skiing, Maggie Loring
Snowboarding, Julia Carlson
Winter Sports, Iseult Devlin

• •

Ragged Mountain Press

A Division of The McGraw-Hill Companies

10 9 8 7 6 5 4 3 2 1
Copyright © 2001 Ragged Mountain Press
All rights reserved. The publisher takes no responsibility for the use of any of the materials or methods described in this book, nor for the products thereof. The name "Ragged Mountain Press" and the Ragged Mountain Press logo are trademarks of The McGraw-Hill Companies. Printed in the United States of America.

Cataloging-in-Publication Data is on file with the Library of Congress

Questions regarding the content of this book should be addressed to
Ragged Mountain Press
P.O. Box 220
Camden, ME 04843
www.raggedmountainpress.com

Questions regarding the ordering of this book should be addressed to
The McGraw-Hill Companies
Customer Service Department
P.O. Box 547
Blacklick, OH 43004
Retail customers: 1-800-262-4729
Bookstores: 1-800-722-4726

Printed on 70-pound Citation by Quebecor Printing Company, Fairfield, PA
Design by Carol Inouye, Inkstone Communications Design
Illustrations by Elayne Sears except for pages 46 and 50 by Accurate Art
Production management by Janet Robbins
Page layout by Shannon Swanson
Edited by Alice M. Bennett

Photographs by Heidi Sell unless otherwise noted: pages 54, 87 (bottom), and 89 (top) courtesy P. Bianchi; page 115 courtesy BizGolf Dynamics; page 26 courtesy Canyon Ranch; page 111 courtesy Corbis; pages 97 and 99 courtesy J.D. Cuban; pages 11, 27, 30, 45, 54, 81, 85, 94 (top), 113, 119 (top), 121, 129 and 131 courtesy Digital Stock; pages 122 and 125 courtesy Krista Dunton; pages 59 and 60 courtesy *Golf Magazine*/Fred Vuich; pages 53 and 127 courtesy The King and the Bear World Golf Village; page 43 courtesy Lady Fairway; pages 37 (bottom) and 40 courtesy Nancy Lopez Golf; page 124 courtesy LPGA; page 92 courtesy Anthony Neste; pages 38 and 41 courtesy Ping; page 90 courtesy Charlie Samuels; page 19 courtesy Singing Hills Resort; page 39 courtesy Square Two Golf; page 88 courtesy Sun Mountain; page 40 (top) courtesy Top Flite

Callaway, Dunlop, Golf For Women, Lady Fairway, Ping, Pinnacle, Rave, Spalding, Square Two, Titleist, Top Flite, and Wilson are registered trademarks.

• •

To Patricia Sinnett Flammer

• •

• •

"Even when you've been playing for five years, like I have, there are days when you go out to play and can't do anything right. That's when you go back to basics. Golf can be frustrating, but it can also be the most fun thing in the world. Just remember, even the pros have bad days. Then there are days when you go out and everything falls into place and you'll have an exceptionally good round. Never let the game get you down, and always, always, always have fun."

—Janet Black, grandmother and avid golfer

• •

CONTENTS

CONTENTS

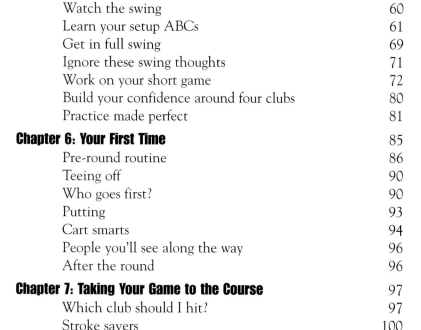
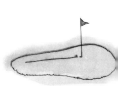

Acknowledgments

It's hard to know where to begin. The opportunity to write this book would not have existed had my husband, Michael Davis, not introduced me nearly a decade ago to this sport he loves so much. He has patiently mentored me ever since, from my first whiff to my first birdie, for which I am deeply grateful.

I'm also grateful to Leslie Day Craige, the editor-in-chief of *Golf for Women* magazine, for believing in me and for supporting my role in this project. I want to thank my editor at Ragged Mountain Press, Molly Mulhern Gross, for her patience, flexibility, and encouragement every step of the way.

I did not write this book alone. It's with tremendous gratitude that I acknowledge Krista Dunton, Katherine Marren, Heidi Bianchi, and the many women—from the wonderful teaching professionals I've met through my job at the magazine to my friends and family who love the game as much as I do—who took the time to share their expertise and golf experiences with me. Their collective wisdom is found throughout these pages. My thanks also to Heidi Sell for taking such wonderful photos.

I also want to thank my sister, Priscilla Fitzsimmons, who took up the game as I wrote the book and provided much inspiration for it.

Most importantly, I am so grateful to my mother, Patricia Sinnett Flammer, for having shared her love of the game with me and for all the wonderful times we spent on the golf course together, experiences I will forever cherish.

Chapter 1

TEN HABITS OF HIGHLY SUCCESSFUL GOLFERS

Golf is a lifetime adventure with you as the star. There are thrills ("I got the ball in the air! I broke 100!"), alien forces ("I could putt yesterday!"), and scary moments in the spotlight ("I have to tee off in front of all these people?").

"Golfer" is a demanding role, and there's no understudy. There is, however, a big supporting cast to help you learn the game, with all its quirky traditions and etiquette. The fun is up to you.

For three and a half years I've played a supporting role at *Golf For Women* magazine by writing and editing stories aimed at helping women to start playing, improve, and have fun golfing. But that's not how my own golf adventure began. When my boyfriend—now husband—gave me a set of golf clubs and a week at golf school for Christmas eight years ago, I never imagined that I had stumbled into the fastest-growing sport among women. (For number crunchers, the latest statistics from the National Golf Foundation [NGF] say there are 5+ million women golfers out of some 26 million players and that women and juniors make up the fastest-growing segment of the sport.)

> "**P**laying nine holes is the ideal way for me to keep a foot in the game."
>
> —Karen Moraghan, owner, Hunter Public Relations, 25+ handicap

"It was almost like starting all over when I began playing golf again. Yet my swing returned, and so did the childhood lessons like 'brush the ground on your backswing.' My love of the game returned as well, pleasant memories evoked by golf's magic moments: the smell of freshly mown fairways, the sound of a well-struck ball, sprinklers coming on at dusk, fresh footprints on a dewy morning."

—Cori Kenicer, golf and travel writer, 23 handicap

Even more than eight years ago, today golf is the sport to play. It has emerged from its fuddy-duddy image to become hip, hot, and happening. *In Style* magazine has devoted pages to fashionable golf duds—Prada and Tommy Hilfiger are just two of the top designers who offer golf apparel. Celebrities from Celine Dion, who owns her own course in Montreal, to soccer superstar Mia Hamm (who shoots in the 80s and dreams of one day becoming a golf pro), are addicted. And in just three months my once tennis-obsessed sister has become a golfing maniac. We used to talk on the phone about my niece's and nephews' triumphs in tennis and Little League, but now she calls to tell me she shot 105 and missed making her first birdie by two inches.

Just as quickly as some get hooked, however, others become disenchanted. For one thing, it's not like skiing, where you can hit the slopes and see signs of progress the very first day. Developing sound golf skills takes time—and infinite patience. One minute you think you've got it; the next, the alien forces take over and you're convinced you're the most uncoordinated person on earth. Whenever these rogue emotions take over, remember there's never been an expert who didn't start out as a rank novice.

Turning more people away from the game than the issue of skill, according to the NGF, are time and cost. It's particularly hard for many women to carve out four hours—the average time it takes to play an eighteen-hole round—while balancing work and family

"I think because I started the game so young, at age 6, I don't have the hesitation that some adult beginners have. However, this doesn't mean I'm not nervous every time I step up to the first tee. That moment when you feel the grip of your driver is always intimidating. It wasn't until recently that I began spending time on the range warming up before a round. I couldn't believe the difference it made in my confidence level. I play about thirty rounds a year."

—Amy DiAdamo, 20-something, avid golfer

• •

"Time is the toughest issue with women because they always have so much going on in their lives. Go out and play nine holes late in the day when you're not taking up such a big chunk of time. Let golf be the time for you to relax, to let out stress, to get exercise, build friendships, and enjoy a great game! Find friends who love to play or join a league or a club to meet new people who play. Golfers are very passionate and love to share the game with others, so it's never hard to find people with a similar interest."

—Krista Dunton, LPGA and PGA teaching professional

• •

life. But you don't have to play golf that way. You can play nine holes or fewer, and you can practice effectively in your living room or backyard. In short, you can create your own golf experience without becoming a card-carrying member of the United States Golf Association (USGA).

And yes, you can easily plunk down $1,500 or more for a set of golf clubs and pay $300 for a round at a swanky resort. But you can also buy a good set of clubs for $300, and the average green fee for a weekend round of golf at an eighteen-hole municipal course in the United States is $27.

At the magazine we hear more about women having trouble finding playing partners (there are lots of leagues for women; see chapter 9). Others cite the umpteen rules (thirty-four, to be exact) as intimidating (you need to know only a few to get going; see chapter 8). And unfortunately, most women at some point will feel they're not always welcome on the golf course. This discrimination can be subtle: a group of guys is allowed to tee off before you even though you had an earlier starting time, or the guy in the golf shop says that the women's clubs, a minuscule collection, are over there in the "pink" department. Or it can be blatant: forbidding women to become members of certain private clubs—an astonishing practice in this day and age.

Why don't I play as much as I'd like to? I live in New York City. But even that's not a good excuse any more. America's cities are being transformed into gigantic playgrounds. Living in Manhattan, I can thwack golf balls at Chelsea Piers, a five-story driving range, take a lesson at a golf store two stories above Madison Avenue, or ride the subway to one of the city's 13 municipal golf courses. And outside urban areas, access is not an issue. In 2000, 300 courses opened—80 percent of them public—and there are 1,500 more new ones in the pipeline.

Whatever may have stopped you from trying the game or from playing it as often as you'd like, here's a ten-step action plan for turning your budding interest in golf into a lifetime commitment. And lifetime is no exaggeration. At *Golf For Women* we've written about ninety-year-old Margaret Dewberry, who plays golf every day in her hometown of Augusta, Georgia, and recently shot her age—quite an accomplishment.

1. Make a commitment— to yourself

Many women and girls take up the sport, as I did, because a boyfriend, husband, father, or boss wants them to. That's a fine inspiration, but you must play because you want to play. As teaching pro Melissa Whitmire of the Ladies Professional Golf Association (LPGA) says, "You need to have a deep, heartfelt purpose for playing to be successful." I was addicted to learning something new and had plenty of motivation and desire of my own. And I still do.

Once you make that commitment to yourself, find a time in your schedule when you can carve out about ten to twelve weeks during which you will take a lesson at least once a week—and practice a few hours between lessons. Commit to this process of developing your skills before you decide whether or not to stick with the game.

"**W**hat's kept me in the game is recognizing that this is something I do in my leisure time; though I aspire to do it well, it's something I'm choosing to do, not something I have to do. It also helps to know that this is a sport I can play for a long time, and it sure beats sitting down eating junk food. I've been playing for ten seasons and play nine holes twice a week with my husband. As a beginner I feared making a fool of myself, and I still do today. My fear has been lessened slightly by realizing that other golfers don't care what your game looks like because they're struggling with their own."

—Dr. Deborah Bright, author and stress management expert

2. Find a guardian angel

Playing with people who are better than you helps you become a better player. Your golf guardian, or mentor, can be your mom, a friend, a spouse, or a partner. Mine was my husband. Your guardian should not be a teaching professional (imagine the bill!) but rather a regular playing partner who can clue you in on the nuances of the game—observing its common courtesies, driving a cart, speeding up play, understanding the lingo, and learning the traditions and rituals. To a beginner, this information is often more valuable than the mechanics of the swing.

3. Don't take free advice

Golfers are a friendly bunch and love to "help" beginners, dispensing tips whether asked for them or not. Women are highly susceptible to this behavior. Not all golf tips apply to you or your swing, and there are dozens of teaching methods, often contradictory. I think golf magazines should add a caveat to each article that says, "Consult your teaching professional before trying this tip."

In short, learn to recognize what's right for you, and take lessons from a pro, who will get you golfing better faster. Education is the best investment you can make for your golfing longevity, and working on proper form will also help you stay injury-free. (See chapter 2 for how to find a golf pro and how to take a lesson.)

4. Practice, and make it meaningful

Develop your skills! As teaching pro Melissa Whitmire says, "You need a good foundation, or the house is going to crumble." I can't think of any other sport where this is so apropos. Golf professionals are always going back to the basics to keep their swings on track. To maintain your swing, the checkpoints should be few (maybe one or two), exact, perfectly clear, and appropriate to you. You must also devote practice time to all the strokes in golf, from putting to chipping to the full swing (see chapter 5).

5. Say no to hand-me-down clubs

Treat yourself to equipment that fits your swing and body. I still can't believe the number of women who say, "Oh, any old club will do for now." Not true. If you use clubs that are too heavy or stiff, you'll be starting out at a disadvantage. The women's equipment market is in an upswing, and there are plenty of professionals who can measure you for a proper set of clubs without breaking the bank (see chapter 3, Gearing Up).

"The most challenging part of the game for me is finding the time to practice. I need serious practice time to get better."

—Tara Gravel, associate editor,
Golf Magazine

"Never, never, never let your husband teach you to play golf. Always take lessons from a golf professional. And never give up! Even when you've been playing for five years like I have, there are days when you go out to play and can't do anything right. That's when you go back to basics. Golf can be frustrating, but it can also be the most fun thing in the world. Just remember, even the pros have bad days. Then there are days when you go out and everything falls into place and you'll have an exceptionally good round. Never let the game get you down, and always, always, always have fun."

—Janet Black, grandmother and avid golfer

6. Set specific, attainable, and measurable goals

Okay, duh. But like anything in life, do set goals. Recognize that golf is a challenging game that will take some dedication (read practice) before you'll see improvement. Manage your expectations and set your goals according to your skill level.

7. Learn to play with your significant other

This may be the most important lesson you take away from this book. Too many golfing relationships have been spoiled by well-meaning spouses giving inappropriate advice. To learn how to lay the ground rules, see the section on couples' golf in chapter 2.

8. Take baby steps

"There are many reasons I love golf, but you *don't* have enough time to hear all of them, so I'll only give you a few. First is the fact that you do not have to be a certain size, shape, or age to play. Second, my husband and I can spend quality time together while enjoying the outdoors. Last but certainly not least is the pure excitement of being part of something that enables women to excel in a sport and be just as good as her brother, husband, or father!"

—Heidi Olschefski-Lusby, an avid new golfer

Stay away from playing eighteen or even nine holes on a busy course until you are ready. This may sound curmudgeonly, but you will be much happier if you stay off the course until you've built a solid foundation. Your lessons should expose you to the course and the object of the game, but I see far too many people playing golf who can't make contact with the ball. There's

"I always start a beginner with putting. I want them to know that golf is about getting the ball in the hole, and I want them to establish that perspective and become 'hole friendly' from their first experience. You can explain and experience golf on the putting green, from the rules and etiquette to the order and pace of play to scoring—you name it. Also there is the advantage of starting with a small motion that then leads to chipping that leads to pitching that leads to full swings. I think it's a travesty when a beginner only gets full swing instruction with a 7-iron."

—Lynn Marriott, golf educator and cofounder of Coaching for the Future golf schools, Phoenix, Arizona

THE OATH OF GOLF HAPPINESS

Before you begin your golf journey, please take a moment to read and sign this oath written by LPGA teaching professional and former LPGA Tour player Melissa Whitmire. Whitmire leads Positive Strokes golf schools (which include swing fundamentals as well) in Greensboro, North Carolina. See chapter 10, Resources, for information on how to reach her.

I _____ do cheerfully swear that:
I will play golf for the sheer joy of the experience of the game.
That I will not, under any circumstances
(shank nor 3-putt nor quadruple bogey)
Throw my club, curse at God,
Or threaten to harm myself or my spouse.
Rather, I will appreciate the opportunity to
Test my physical skills and emotional stability.
That I will celebrate the glorious feelings
That arise during the playing of a round:
Rage, joy, despair, disgust, hope, frustration, determination, and elation.
That I will cherish the companionship of my friends and family
(and be someone whom they will cherish as well).
That I will take the time to soak in
The natural beauty of the golf course, to smell the roses
(even if they are out of bounds in somebody's back yard!)
and enjoy the fresh air and sunshine.
I love this game and promise that no matter what happens
I will remember that
Golf is a game, not a life threatening experience!
Yes, I _____ do cheerfully swear
To play and have fun for all the days of my golfing life.

— © Melissa Whitmire, *Happiness in Golf*

"The one quality women need to succeed in golf is a sense of humor."

—Judy Bell, consulting director, USGA Foundation

nothing more frustrating to you or to the players around you. Waiting will pay off with a higher satisfaction level and a better chance of sticking with the game. As in skiing, you start on the bunny slopes; you wouldn't attempt black-diamond runs on day one. If you can't resist playing a round, book a tee time at an off-hour on a weekday and play just a few holes with your golf guardian.

• •

"I have a routine. I play once a week (even if it's just nine holes), and I practice at least twice a week. If, however, I feel golf is becoming a burden or chore, I stop practicing. There's really nothing worse than hitting ball after ball if my heart isn't in it. After a while, however, I remember why I love the game and quickly get back into my routine. I love to play with my husband, and I especially like to play with his buddies when I can. Playing with the guys gives me the challenge of wanting to play well, and I usually do."

—Terri Leonard, author of *In the Women's Clubhouse*, four-year player, handicap 20

• •

9. Get in golf shape

Golf is a sport, and women need to think of it this way, says Dede Braun, director of instruction at Crystal Springs Golf Course in Burlingame, California. Braun, who leads golf clinics called Golf Divas, teaches fitness (strength training, cardiac endurance, and flexibility) as a key component of a good golf game. Bigger and stronger and flexible can mean more shots that go longer on the course. (See chapter 7 for fitness tips and exercises.)

10. Keep it fun

You must learn to enjoy the game regardless of how you play. To that end, please read and sign the Oath of Golf Happiness on the previous page. "You are not your golf swing and you are not your golf score, so don't attach your self-worth to whether you get the ball airborne," says Whitmire, who wrote the oath to inspire her students. And don't defer happiness until you reach your goals: "I'd be so happy if I could break 100." "I'd love this game if only I could putt." Don't go there!

You of course will need to map out your own plan for success—there's no secret formula—but if you follow at least some of the advice above, I think you'll find that although it'll take some time to get it right, golf's joys far outweigh its challenges. Good golfing!

• •

"I always remind myself of the joy of the game even if I have a few bad holes."

—Lucretia Bingham, forty-year player, handicap "somewhere around 20"

• •

Chapter 2

LESSON PLAN

I don't do ball sports," declares my great friend Beth Howard, who has competed in the Eco-Challenge and excels at just about every adventure sport there is. Yet one of her favorite pastimes for burning up her abundant energy is to go to a driving range and smack balls with a driver. She doesn't care if she whiffs, and she's not afraid to attack the ball. Does she enjoy "golf"? Yes. Does she need to take lessons? No. I, on the other hand, want and need lessons because I'm serious about getting better. I play golf for my job and aspire to play in a competitive league (some day!). So should you gear up for golf lessons? The answer is a definite "yes" if you check off any of the reasons below:

- you want to not whiff the ball at the corporate outing

- you want to start golfing or golf more often

- you want to preserve your longevity in the sport—and your sanity

- you want to add another dimension to the family vacation

- you want to make a serious commitment to the game

- you want to improve your business relationships

- you want to stay injury free

- you want to take years off the learning curve

- you want to have fun!

Whether you're a new golfer or a budding Babe Zaharias, lessons are a good thing. As in all sports, the purpose is to get you started off right, and it's a small investment for a game you can play well into your eighties, or longer. Time and desire—not age, shape, or athletic ability—are the most important assets in getting good at the game.

Your goals will determine your approach to lessons. Find a learning environment that matches your objectives. If you want to be on the fast track to improvement, you have to commit to some regular lessons with the same pro, and you need to be honest about your practice habits.

PRIVATE LESSONS: THE FASTEST WAY TO SUCCESS

With the one-on-one attention you'll receive in a private lesson, you can have almost instant gratification in getting the ball airborne. "It's not hard to get a beginner to hit the ball in the air in the first lesson," says Dede Braun, director of instruction at Crystal Springs Golf Course in Burlingame, California. "Students' reactions are often a whoop or shriek of pure pleasure. They can't believe it's that easy. I figure that's part of being a golf teacher—to get that hook in right away."

It's a good idea to develop a relationship with one teacher. She or he will help you choose the right equipment and monitor your development as a player—going over rules, etiquette, and scoring strategies as well as the swing fundamentals. A good pro will also give you warm-up exercises to avoid injury, provide mental game tips to conquer first-tee jitters—in other words, she'll treat the whole golfer in you.

An instructor will also help you set reasonable goals based on your available time, commitment level, and practice habits. Your goals may not be realistic because of limited time or physical capacity (not everyone can hit the ball over 200 yards).

"At the completion of the lesson, write down in your own words what you learned during the session. Have your instructor check your notes and add any important information you have omitted. Be sure to include any drills and how to perform them. Take the time to practice the drills between each lesson. They will help you learn the new feeling faster."

—Jackie Bertram Kaufman, lead instructor, Nicklaus/Flick Golf Schools, and director of instruction, TPC at Heron Bay

A teacher needs to have high expectations of your ability and potential, and you want to find a pro who enjoys working with new golfers. Many women are immediately assigned to an assistant pro, who may lack interest or experience in dealing with beginners or women.

The downside? Private lessons aren't cheap. They typically cost from $30 to $75 an hour. In a busy metropolitan area like New York, however, you can pay $100 or more. And a name-brand instructor at a top facility can charge hundreds for his or her time.

> It's ideal to take lessons where you plan to practice and play. Most teaching pros camp out on the lesson tee all day, and they may stroll by while you're practicing, so you may get free tips.

How many lessons will you need to get going? "My beginners can hit the ball fairly solidly after six to ten lessons, although everyone is unique," says Deb Steinbach, a former LPGA Tour pro who teaches at the Reserve in Palm Springs, California, and specializes in women golfers. Braun suggests at least three lessons to nail down grip, posture, alignment, and the basic swing motion.

Finding a Pro

Anyone can hang up a shingle and call herself a teaching pro. Look for someone who is a certified member of either the Ladies Professional Golf Association's Teaching and Club Professional division or the Professional Golfers' Association of America (PGA; see chapter 10, Resources). These credentials virtually guarantee the person has been trained to teach—the LPGA is particularly good at grooming instructors. Many of these pros have had competitive playing experience as well, as either amateurs or professionals, which can be an asset on the lesson tee, particularly for more advanced students.

Locating a qualified pro is easy. It's rare to find a golf facility that doesn't have a resident instructor. Professionals at private country clubs typically can give lessons to nonmembers. Golf resorts, driving ranges, and public courses all are good places to start your search. I've even had a lesson in a New York City golf shop, hitting balls into a net. It's ideal, however, to take lessons where you plan to practice and play. Most teaching pros camp out on the lesson tee all day, and they may stroll by while you're practicing, so you may get free tips.

As with any professional service (haircuts, for example!), get a referral and talk with the pro before you sign on for a series of lessons. You may have to go to several instructors before you find one who's right for you. "The pro's personality, availability, and lesson schedule need to match yours," advises Katherine Marren, PGA member and senior instructor at Pebble Beach Golf Academy in Pebble Beach, California. Here are some ideas about what to ask a potential teacher.

- What are her rates? Is there a discount for a series of lessons? Will she give semiprivate lessons (a good cost-cutting measure)?

- What are her credentials, and what levels of golfers does she work with? Has she worked with beginners and women before?

- Will she take you out on the golf course for a playing lesson, where you will learn game strategy, club selection, and how to hit different types of shots?

- How long will she or he be in the area? Pros move around a good bit or divide their time between facilities. Many in the north fly south for the winter.

- Does she teach a "method"? Be aware that one swing theory does not fit all. Teaching styles and learning preference should match up. If you love games and imagery, find a pro who teaches that way.

Is a woman pro a better choice for you?

I've had both men and women instructors and have had good experiences with both. Some experts feel it's smart to have a lesson from someone who can serve as a swing model. There are strength issues women face that some men can't relate to. And of course there are breasts. What do you do with them? If you're well endowed, you have to feel comfortable asking for tips on maneuvering around them.

GOLF SCHOOLS: A CRASH COURSE

I'd been playing golf for about three years, mostly on vacation or when visiting my parents. I wasn't getting any better—for one thing, I never practiced. My solution? A week at golf camp.

Schools are fun, supportive environments that can help you jump-start your efforts and instill good habits. I got a written evaluation of my swing, with a few key thoughts and drills, plus a manual, and the pro gave the five of us in the group her home phone number in case we had any questions. Today most schools send you home with a video of your swing.

The program I attended was a five-day total immersion golf experience. We were in "class" from 9:00 till 4:00, then we could go out and play on the course. We hit tons of balls, and I collapsed into bed at 8:00 every night. There are many, many programs, from a day to a week, offering everything from the total immersion experience I had to introductory "golf lite" programs at cushy resorts where you can not only perfect your swing but unwind with a hot stone massage and a margarita. More and more schools are designed for women, and a growing number have a business focus that covers rules and etiquette—a great timesaving tool if your golf experience will be limited to a few rounds a year with your clients.

Costs vary greatly, from a few hundred dollars to a few thousand, and packages generally include instruction, meals, lodging, and green fees. Many programs are at spots with enough vacation appeal for a nongolfing spouse. But you don't have to hop on a plane to attend one. Look locally. There are many innovative teachers out there who run fun and effective two- and three-

• •

"I believe private lessons are almost always the most effective way to begin. I say *almost*, since some women learn and enjoy the experience more in a social setting. Private lessons allow the instructor to thoroughly interview the woman beginner and tailor her learning to her right from the 'get-go.' From that point the learning can be more efficient and productive."

—Lynn Marriott, golf educator and cofounder of Coaching for the Future golf schools, Phoenix, Arizona

• •

day programs. One of my favorites (it must be because of the name) is Golf Divas, a three-day school run by Dede Braun and Angie Papangellin meant to empower and inspire women new to the game. The program covers rules, golf exercises, equipment, nutrition, and scoring and swing basics.

The downside of golf schools? You can go into information overload, and what you learn will begin to fade in a matter of days unless you apply it through consistent practice once you get back home.

Ten things to ask before you sign up for golf school

1. Will you be grouped with students of similar skill level? All women? If you're a beginner and your husband's a Tiger Woods wannabe, look for a school that accommodates both levels.

2. What is the student-to-teacher ratio? Three or four to one is ideal for new golfers. How much one-on-one instruction? Will you get out on the golf course to play with an instructor? Will you have access to the teacher after class or at meals? (These are the times for the "stupid" questions you didn't want to ask in front of everyone else.)

3. What will be covered in the program? Look for a school that covers rules and etiquette, equipment evaluations, on-course experience, and fitness.

4. Will you be given a manual or a personalized practice program? Instruction should not stop when you leave the school.

5. What's the day like? How many hours of instruction? How much leisure time? Will you have access to a golf course? Some programs are half a day so you have time for other pursuits.

6. How did past students like the program? Would they return? Ask for references.

WOMEN'S GOLF SCHOOLS

If you're more comfortable in a women-only classroom, check out these top golf schools that offer special programs for women.

School of Golf for Women
Singing Hills Resort
3007 Dehesa Rd.
El Cajon CA 92019
888-764-4566; 619-442-3425
www.singinghills.com

Pine Needles Golfari
1005 Midland Rd.
Southern Pines NC 28388
800-747-7272
www.rossresorts.com

Marlene Floyd's "For Women
  Only" Golf School
5350 Clubhouse Lane
Hope Mills NC 28348
800-637-2694
www.marlenefloyd.com

Coaching for the Future
  with Lynn Marriott
  and Pia Nilsson
Legacy Golf Resort
6808 S. 32nd St.
Phoenix AZ 85040
888-828-FORE (888-828-3673);
  602-305-5550
www.coachingforthefuture.com

Golf Divas
Crystal Springs Golf Course
6650 Golf Course Dr.
Burlingame CA 94010-6598
650-342-4188, x33

Craft-Zavichas Golf School
600 Dittmer
Pueblo CO 81005
800-858-9633
www.czgolfschool.com

See chapter 10, Resources, for more information on golf schools.

7.   What's covered in the price? Some programs are commuter courses, where you're on your own for lodging and meals. If lodging is included, ask what the accommodations are like. The degree of luxury can vary quite a bit.

8.   Is there an indoor practice area in case of rain?

9.   Do you need clubs, or will they be provided?

10.   Would a nongolfer be happy coming along? Is the place all right for singles or geared more toward vacationing couples?

GROUP LESSONS: THE BEST VALUE

Group lessons—typically offered as a series spread out over a few weeks—are the most budget-friendly way to try out a sport you're curious about. Expect to pay anywhere from $100 to $180 for a series of five or six lessons. The setting is relaxed and social; you may be grouped with five to ten other students—maybe more. It's a great way to meet future playing partners and to realize that you're not the only one who hits bad shots.

"In a lesson format (not on your own on a busy Saturday morning), get on the course as soon as possible so you know how to apply what you're doing and to get firsthand experience of the rules and etiquette. Chip and putt with the goal in mind of getting the ball in the hole in the least number of strokes—the object of the game! In your lessons there should also be a proper emphasis on playing all the shots. For example, putting is more than 40 percent of the game. Treat it like that when you practice."

—Becky Dengler, LPGA and PGA teaching professional,
Ed Oliver Golf Course, Wilmington, Delaware

Often geared to less-experienced players, group lessons tend to give you a broad overview, touching on many areas of the game. Troy Beck, director of instruction at Glenn Dale Golf Club in Maryland, offers a variety of innovative group programs. She has a more traditional one where you review the basics of the swing, but she also gives walking lessons, where you go several holes with an instructor to learn basic etiquette and protocol and how to keep up the speed of play.

A pitfall is that you may be grouped with players of different skill levels, and you will not receive as much one-on-one attention as in a private lesson. "Beginners" come in many guises, from someone who has never held a club to not-so-new-golfers who've been playing for quite a while. (For some reason many women—including me—describe themselves as beginners even if they've been playing for years.)

THE ROLE AND TIMING OF LESSONS

To try out the sport, commit to a ten- to twelve-week period during which you take six to ten lessons with practice sessions in between. If you just want to use golf for the occasional

ARE GOLF SCHOOLS GOOD FOR BEGINNERS?

I don't really recommend golf schools for beginners unless the entire group is beginners. The challenge with this is that women tend to enjoy learning as beginners in a group setting ... less intimidating! A good alternative is small-group clinics or schools designated for beginners. The other challenge with this is that a lot of women golfers consider themselves beginners even if they have played for many years, so ... I used to call the clinics "*beginner*-beginner" clinics and then the women knew what was being offered.

—Lynn Marriott

• •

"**I** want to get new golfers on the golf course ASAP! Again this is what it's all about
. . . *playing golf!* Often with a "beginner-beginner" group we will walk a golf hole
in the first lesson or session, again so they start to establish a relationship to what
they are learning. I will play the hole and explain what I am doing and ask for
questions. If the school or clinic has the time built in, I always want to end with
the experience of playing golf. If the instruction is presented in the right order,
new golfers can get out on the golf course right away. They will know to pick up
their ball if they are holding up play, but they really need to experience *golf*."

—Lynn Marriott

• •

More and more golf schools are designed for
women, and a growing number have a business
focus that covers rules and etiquette.

business round, that will be more than enough to launch your efforts.

Consider the time of year. Will you have opportunities to play and practice? I wish I'd timed my golf school stint closer to springtime, when golf season begins in New York. Since I attended in December, I went about three months without playing. When scheduling your lessons, think about the time of day. You don't want to arrive stressed or have to cancel because of work or family obligations. You might still be charged if you don't show up. And budget time immediately after the lesson to practice—even if it's only 10 to 15 minutes, this will help you retain what you learned.

Practice doesn't have to occur on the golf course. You can work on your golf swing at home, without a golf ball. Use the time you're watching TV to establish a grip. Use the backyard for chipping practice and the office floor for grooving a putting stroke.

Will you have a more experienced friend or relative to guide you and play with you—to become your golf mentor? Professionals can take you only so far (and they cost money), and there's plenty of information about the rules and rituals, customs and nuances that you don't need to know right away but can learn as you go. A mentor can show you the ropes. My husband did this.

Manage your expectations. There's no shame in being a beginner. It takes a few months to build a full golf swing; start slowly and you'll gradually achieve success. And don't try to duplicate your lesson while you're playing; use the practice range for that.

PLAYING GOLF WITH YOUR HUSBAND

Playing golf with your mate needn't end your golf career—or your marriage. Fred Shoemaker and his wife, Johanne Hardy, lead workshops for golfing couples. Here the two offer some of their survival tips.

Good Golf for Couples

It seems men can't resist giving their wives golf tips. Unchecked, this behavior can sour many a golfing relationship. I often see women being given instruction by their husbands, and the experience has a low learning outcome. If the woman can't immediately execute the instruction she's just been given, she may start feeling the pressure to perform, not wanting to disappoint her husband. She may be so embroiled in this that she can't pay attention to her swing. In this environment she will learn very little.

Often when the husband sees little result from his first tip, he may give his wife another, and another. At some point his wife may be trying to remember, incorporate, and execute three or four things. She's so busy—even stressed—trying to juggle and remember all these things that she can't feel the swing variations that would lead to learning. After one or a few such lessons she may walk away believing she has no chance at golf and may give up on it altogether.

I have given many workshops to couples about coaching each other. I encourage women to create a partnership for learning with their husbands, the key to which is establishing some ground rules and sticking to them. The most radical notion is this: the student (in this case, the woman) asks to be coached and sets the agenda; the coach (the man) must coach only when asked and stick to that agenda in an objective way. For example, let's say the wife asks to be coached on the length of her backswing. The husband then will serve as a pair of eyes to help confirm what she experienced. She swings, then says, "I felt that the club went all the way to parallel at the top." (The student always speaks first.) The husband then responds with what he saw. "It was a foot short of parallel." That's all, and that's good coaching.

When people step outside these bounds and make judgments and suggestions, things start to fall apart.

—Fred Shoemaker

(continued next page)

PLAYING GOLF WITH YOUR HUSBAND

(continued from previous page)

How and Why It Works

Although I didn't know how to ask for coaching when I started playing golf six years ago, I was lucky enough to have a partner (Fred) wise enough to set effective learning guidelines.

When Fred coaches me it's not about him measuring himself as a coach by how well I hit the ball. We set up an environment that's clearly about my learning. I don't have to worry about performing for him, and that frees me up to learn and be aware of what's happening in my swing. Mishits are part of learning, and I have the freedom to mishit without wondering if he's okay with those shots.

Since Fred and I agree that he needs a clear invitation to coach me, I have the freedom to explore without worrying that he'll jump in when I'm right in the middle of something that fascinates me. I also know that when I request coaching, I can specify what area I want to explore and know I won't be overwhelmed with information. It's clear and simple: I choose an area I want feedback on, and this is the area on which he provides it. Period.

It makes sense for me to decide when and if I want coaching, because I know when I'm ready to expand my awareness to a new area. Besides, some days I'm just not up to being coached. I may be more interested in being outdoors or exploring something on my own.

These rules of coaching have enabled me to create a learning environment that works for me as a student. And it does: I have developed quickly, and I love playing golf with, and being coached by, my husband.

—Johanne Hardy

Fred Shoemaker is the coauthor of Extraordinary Golf: The Art of the Possible *and the founder and head coach of School for Extraordinary Golf, Carmel, California. Johanne Hardy manages the school and is now a member of the coaching team.*

"**H**ave you ever watched what happens when a woman practices by herself on the driving range? I think she has an invisible sign on her back that says, 'No matter what I say or do, please give me a golf tip!' There are two ways to thwart this behavior: The first is to let advisers know that you're exploring something specific and would like to stay with that. The other is to hand them your 5-iron and request that they hit the 175-yard marker. If they can't, let them know you're passing on the lesson!"

—Fred Shoemaker, School for Extraordinary Golf, Carmel, California

LESSON SUMMARY

Golf is one of the few sports (the only one?) that you learn off the playing field. You learn tennis on the court, swimming in the pool, snowboarding on the slopes. In golf it's typically the practice range. Look for a teacher or a program that will help you bridge the gap between the practice tee and the golf course by incorporating the playing experience in lessons, so you can quickly see the big picture and experience the fun of it.

As LPGA master instructor Annette Thompson likes to say, "Just because you can type doesn't mean you can write. It's the same thing in golf. Just because you can swing a club doesn't mean you can play the game."

• •

AVOIDING INFORMATION OVERLOAD

As a new golfer, you'll be tempted to read every magazine and book, watch every video, and accept every tip that comes your way (and there will be plenty). Learn to discern what's right for you, and always talk to a teacher about any drills or tips before you make them part of your game.

• •

And keep in mind that you will always be learning, refining. That's golf. Be prepared for plateaus and for times you'll feel like throwing your hands up in disgust and quitting. But don't get stuck in the "I need to get better to have fun" syndrome: If only I could drive the ball two hundred yards, golf would be so much more fun. If only I could shoot 92, golf would be so much better. Though it is fun to get better, try not to rely on getting better to have fun—enjoy the learning process.

At some point you have to give yourself permission to stop tinkering with your swing and just play. You can play perfectly good golf and have a less than perfect swing. And no matter what, always keep your goal in mind: playing golf, not just perfecting a golf swing!

Chapter 3

GEARING UP

For a good year my sister, with three children in school and a husband who's got the golfing bug, had been thinking about taking up the game. When she finally played her first nine holes with her husband, she used his old set of clubs.

Rookie mistake number one: playing with men's hand-me-downs. Old or new, such clubs are too heavy and stiff-shafted for most women, which can ingrain poor swing habits from the start. They also make the game more difficult than it has to be.

And your granny's old set won't do either. The technology has become so user friendly in the past five years, and with more choices for women, that anything older should have dinosaur status. If you're a skier, think of those parabolic skis that practically escort you down the mountain. Or the oversize tennis rackets that making missing the ball next to impossible. Would you still borrow a wooden tennis racket? As any pro will tell you, the right equipment is an essential part of a good golf swing.

KEEP START-UP COSTS LOW

It's easy to see the appeal of playing with any old thing: you can get started without feeling committed (it seems that women have a huge fear of commitment when it comes to buying golf clubs). Borrowing clubs isn't out of the question, but make sure you get them from a female friend

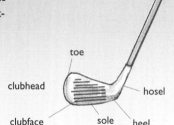

ANATOMY OF A GOLF CLUB

Who knew? Clubs have toes, heels, and faces! All golf clubs have the three basic parts outlined below. It's a good idea to become familiar with these features, because your teaching pro will refer to them often.

The grip, or handle. Grips come in different sizes and can be leather, rubber, or synthetic.

The shaft. The shaft is the part of the club that bends when you hit the ball, and it comes in variable degrees of flexibility. The longer the shaft, the farther the ball is designed to go. Most players, except some tour players who use steel, should look for graphite shafts. The shaft fits into the **hosel**, which joins it to the clubhead.

The clubhead. Lighter materials such as titanium and super steel have enabled clubheads in irons and woods to be made larger, which delivers a bigger effective hitting area and a greater margin of error—that is, the ball will still go pretty dang far if you hit it off-center. Woods, irons, and putters all have distinctly different clubhead designs. All clubheads have three components: the **toe**, **heel**, and **sole**.

grip

shaft

toe

clubhead

hosel

clubface

sole

heel

who's about the same height and strength. Golf clubs, like golfers, come in different sizes.

To keep your investment to a minimum without stinting on quality if you're just testing the waters, here are two more tactics.

Buy a partial set

You'll find "starter sets" (that's how they're labeled) built for beginners that typically include a half set of clubs: often a putter, three irons, and two woods, which is more than enough to get you going. A starter set will run $100 to $250.

These clubs usually have a shorter shaft and more loft (see pages 35–36) than standard clubs to make it easier to hit the ball. But if you outgrow them, you cannot have them adjusted.

"In most cases," says Lorraine Klippel, owner and head professional at Bumble Bee Hollow in

> "Some things just aren't worth skimping on: graphite shafts; stainless steel clubheads; a clubfitting session with a pro."
>
> —Carol Preisinger, 1998 LPGA National Teacher of the Year

ADJUSTING CLUBS

If you already own clubs, have a pro evaluate your equipment to determine whether you need to make swing changes or equipment changes. Just as with a dress or suit, alterations can be made to most clubs.

Mechanicsburg, Pennsylvania, and an expert clubfitter, "the quality of these starter sets isn't high enough. And the sets don't come with clubs new golfers would benefit from most. For example, they often include a 1-wood (a driver) and a 3-wood when beginners would be better off with the higher-lofted 5- and 7-woods." (The more loft a club has, the easier it is to get the ball airborne.)

Rather than buying a starter set, go for the nicest clubs you can afford and buy just a couple to start, suggests Klippel. You only need one lofted fairway wood, such as a 5- or 7-wood; a 6-or 7-iron; either a pitching wedge or a sand wedge; and a putter (see pages 36–39 for definitions of golf clubs).

In the lower price range, it's best to stick with major brands such as Spalding, Dunlop, and Wilson. Wilson Lady Pro Staff Performance is a reliable line of clubs available at national sporting goods stores. Whatever you buy, make sure the clubs have graphite shafts (much lighter than steel and thus easier to swing) and stainless steel clubheads—not a metal-composite alloy, which won't hold up.

In premium and midpriced brands, woods and irons are sold separately and are priced per club. Some stores don't like to sell clubs individually (it makes more work for them), but a reputable store will allow you to buy them this way. What's more, these clubs can be adjusted to fit you if the standard off-the-rack model isn't right.

"If you buy good clubs to begin with you don't need to change unless your swing changes," says Klippel. And if you do outgrow your clubs, higher-end clubs can be altered, just as a tailor would adjust a suit you'd outgrown. If you buy at the low end, you're stuck with what you have.

What price glory? At the higher end, you are buying higher-quality materials such as titanium, which is strong, lightweight, and durable, product warranties, good design features, and the ability to have the clubs adjusted if necessary—a longer shaft or bigger grip, for example.

In top-of-the-line brands such as Callaway, Ping, and Titleist, a set of irons may cost well over $1,000 and each wood $300 to $400. The options for women are somewhat limited within these brands, though Ping has the most, offering ten lie angles, two shaft flexes, and three grip sizes for women (see below for a discussion of these qualities).

There are several companies, however, that specialize in high-quality women's equipment at half that price. Three brands to look for are Nancy Lopez Golf (the LPGA Hall of Fame player actually uses these clubs); Square Two Golf, a company

"I'd rather see a woman buy a few clubs of a premium brand than a full set of low-end clubs."

—Lorraine Klippel, clubfitting expert

that's been making women's clubs for more than twenty years (recently it offered a two-club "sampler" of a driver and a 7-iron for $50—with a lifetime warranty!); and Lange Golf.

Rent clubs

I've had success renting equipment, as I still do every time I go skiing (though the rental fees can add up). It's a great way to try before you buy, and many courses, pro shops, and resorts offer good sets. I recommended this route to my sister for her second golf outing, a corporate event at a resort. She loved the clubs so much she wanted to rush out and buy the very same set. Not so fast, I warned.

Rookie mistake number two: buying a set of clubs without knowing your size.

> "It's much easier to fit a club to a golfer's swing than to fit a golfer's swing to a club."
>
> —Becky Dengler, LPGA and PGA
> teaching professional

SIZING CONSIDERATIONS

Are women's clubs always the best choice for women?

In a word, no. *Might* they be a good choice? Yes. Clubs built for women are typically an inch shorter and more flexible and weigh less than men's clubs of the same model, and they are well suited to most women. (At the high-performance levels—pros, top amateurs—however, female-specific models are rarely used.) But if you are on either end of the size range—short or tall—or are very strong, the standard off-the-rack women's model won't be good for you. Taller women can get in trouble because they are often pointed to men's clubs; yet a tall woman might not be strong enough to handle the stiffer shaft flex these clubs come with. Some women will find the women's clubs too short, the grips too small, the shaft flex too soft. Remember: it's not your gender that matters but your swing speed and ability. There's no denying that the standard models do well for most women. But since standards vary among clubmakers—just as clothing sizes vary by manufacturer—it's crucial to try as many clubs as you can before purchasing a set.

> "I wish I'd been clubfitted. I bought one of the leading brands that cost well over a $1,000 for a set and thought they ought to be good, but I wasn't fitted for them. Since I was a strong player, they put me into men's clubs, which weren't right. I played for years with them. My teaching pro has spent a lot of time undoing the bad habits I developed using the wrong clubs."
>
> —Woman golfer in Colorado

Shaft flex

Flex simply refers to a shaft's ability to bend. As a rule, the slower you swing the club, the more flexible a shaft you will need to get the ball up in the air and flying straight. Swing speed, or club-head speed, is measured in miles per hour with radar or using a little device that attaches to the shaft. Most pros and golf shops have these devices, or you can buy one.

A woman tour professional swings a driver about 90 mph. Tiger Woods swings over 100 mph, the average male about 85. Most women fall somewhere in the 50 to 75 mph range. Graphite shafts, which are lighter than steel, are recommended for swing speeds under 70 mph. Most women's clubs are designed for swing speeds like this and are labeled *L* (ladies) flex. *R* is a regular men's flex and is suitable to stronger women players, but each maker's is a little different.

If you don't know your swing speed, you may be asked how far you hit your different clubs to determine the shaft flex you need.

Club length

Shaft length is related to your height (in general, the taller you are the longer the club, and vice versa), but it doesn't necessarily determine the shaft length you need, since two golfers of the same height could easily have different torso, arm, and leg lengths. What makes you feel comfortable, balanced, and confident standing over the ball is the most important determinant.

Lie angle

Lie angle describes how the sole of the club sits on the ground (see right). Ideally, it should be flat when you are set up to hit the ball (see chapter 5). If the toe of the club is in the air, the lie angle is too upright; if the heel is off the ground, it's too flat. An incorrect lie angle can adversely affect the direction of your ball flight. Most standard lie angles are okay. The fitter (see page 36) should ask you to hit different clubs with different lie angles. Some fitters will skip this step because it takes some time to find the right fit. Insist that they take this measurement, advises clubfitting specialist Becky Dengler.

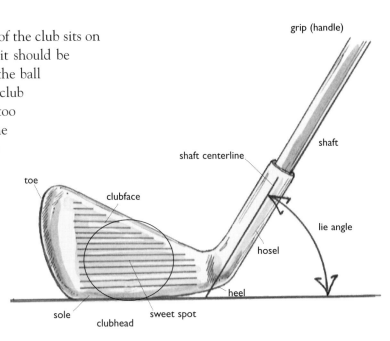

If a club's **lie angle** is too flat or upright, it will make it difficult to hit the ball straight. The best shots result when you hit the club in the **sweet spot**. The goal of a good clubfitting is to get clubs that allow you to do so consistently.

Grip size

Proper *grip size* is easy to determine. Hold the club with your left hand (right-handed golfers have the left hand at the top of the club handle). If your fingertips dig into your palm, the grip is too small. If there's a gap between the palm and fingers, the grip is too big. Your fingertips should graze your palm. A grip that's too big or too small can adversely affect your ability to control the ball's flight.

Loft

Loft is the amount of angle designed into a clubhead to produce a certain trajectory. Loft, expressed in degrees, starts at 8 degrees for a driver and goes all the way to 60 degrees for a lob wedge. The more loft a club has, the higher the ball will go. You should be most concerned about loft

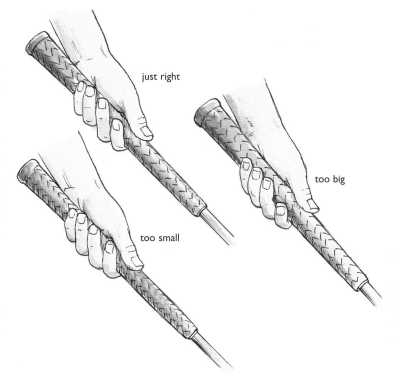

just right

too small

too big

The **grip handle** is the right size if your fingertips graze your palm.

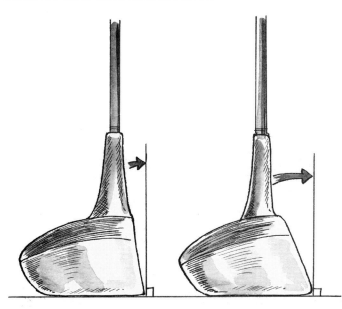

A club's **loft** ranges from 8 degrees in a driver to 60 degrees in a wedge. The higher the loft, the higher the ball will fly. The club on the left has a lower loft than the club on the right, so a shot with the club on the left will not go as high.

"Clubfitting used to mean more time and more money, but not anymore. Clubfitting encourages performance no matter what level you are. There's no way you're going to progress playing with clubs that are too heavy or hard to hit. I still get students who pull out their grandfathers' clubs, which are too heavy, the grips are worn, and the shaft is old. A good fit will minimize mistakes."

—Carol Preisinger

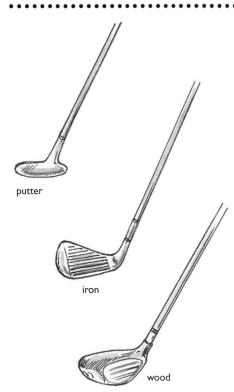

putter

iron

wood

The Rules of Golf allow you to carry up to 14 clubs in your bag—a mix of woods and irons and a putter.

when buying or testing a driver (see the sidebar on page 38, Buying a Driver).

If the club fits, buy it

The best golf shot results when you hit the ball smack in the middle of the clubface (see illustration on page 34). When shopping for clubs, your goal is to find the best combination of loft, flex, length, and grip size that helps you do this consistently.

Few would argue that the ideal way to find clubs that fit your body and your swing is to go through what's known as a *dynamic clubfitting* with a LPGA or PGA teaching professional. These sessions typically take about half an hour, and you will be hitting balls (that's why it's *dynamic*). Most teachers would prefer that you wait for three to six lessons so you are swinging the club with some basic technique before you are fitted.

Many women think they are not good enough players to go through a fitting. Wrong. Properly fitted clubs are more important as you learn and can make the game a lot easier. The cost of a fitting is the same as a golf lesson, and if you buy the clubs from the pro the charge is often credited toward the purchase. The clubs cost the same whether you get fitted for them or not.

Many golf stores offer this service free if you buy the clubs from the store, but the person evaluating you might not be a certified teaching pro, and you'll probably hit into a net, which does not give you the same feedback as outdoors where you can observe your ball flight. Look for a pro who will take all the measurements outlined on pages 34 and 35. Unless they do, they haven't properly fitted you.

WHAT CLUBS DO I NEED?

You are allowed to carry up to fourteen clubs in your bag, according to the Rules of Golf, which are jointly written by the USGA and by the Royal and Ancient Golf Club of St. Andrew's (Scotland). So which clubs should they be? A lot of that depends on your skill level and the type of course you play. A pro can help you decide what clubs you need, and this discussion should be part of any clubfitting session. There are three main categories of clubs: woods, irons, and putters (see illustration previous page). In woods and irons each club is designed to hit the ball a different distance, which is a function of both loft and shaft length. As a rule, the longer the shaft and the less angled (lofted) the clubface, the farther the ball will go.

Woods

First of all, *woods* is a bit of a misnomer, since the heads of these clubs are now made of metal (stainless steel and titanium), so technically this family of clubs is known as *metalwoods*. You'll also hear them referred to as *fairway metals*, because with the exception of the driver (also known as a *1-wood*) these clubs are used primarily from the fairway and the rough. A 3-wood is often used as an alternative to a driver off the tee.

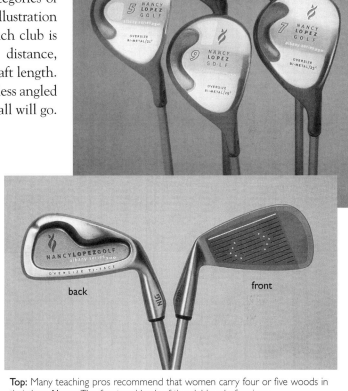

Top: Many teaching pros recommend that women carry four or five woods in their bag. **Above:** The front and back of the clubhead of an iron.

Woods are numbered, starting with the 1-wood (driver) all the way to the 13-wood. As the numbers go up, the loft on the clubface increases and the shafts get shorter.

Because of their larger hitting area and clubhead design, woods are considered easier to hit and get the ball up with than longer irons. Therefore pros often recommend that women carry at least four or five woods in their bags. Lorraine Klippel recommends carrying 3-, 5-, 7-, and 9-woods.

Irons

Irons are numbered from one through nine. One is the longest iron (the shaft is the longest and the loft the lowest among all irons) and is the most difficult to hit. No one except maybe Tiger Woods uses a 1-iron.

BUYING A DRIVER

You may be better off driving with a 3-wood, which has about 16 degrees of loft, but a driver is designed to make the ball roll farther when it lands, usually increasing your distance. If you can hit your 3-wood about 140 yards off the tee, you can definitely swing a driver. But before you buy one, consider these tips from Lorraine Klippel, head professional, Bumble Bee Hollow, Mechanicsburg, Pennsylvania.

What you want from a driver is maximum distance and accuracy. And you need to find a club with the best combination of loft, length, and shaft flex to maximize each.

Loft

The slower your swing, the more loft you need on the club to get the ball in the air. Most women would benefit from using a driver with about 11 to 13 degrees of loft. If you can handle a lower-lofted club such as a 10-degree model, you will benefit from the additional roll it will produce when the ball lands.

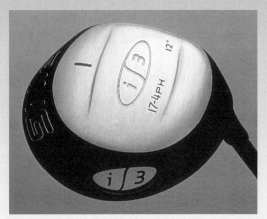

Drivers range in loft from 8 to 13 degrees. For just starting out, choose one with 11 to 13 degrees of loft.

Shaft Flex

Go with a shaft that's as flexible as possible. The slower your swing speed, the more flexible the shaft should be.

Shaft Length

Drivers for women range from 42 to 45 or so inches in length. In theory, the longer the shaft the more clubhead speed you generate, thus the more distance you can create. However, a longer shaft makes it harder to hit the ball accurately and consistently, and you will really benefit from a longer shaft only if you can hit the ball solidly. Shorter shafts will give you a good chance of making a solid, straight hit.

In short, go with a little bit shorter club, say 43 inches, with more loft (11 to 13 degrees) and you will hit it better. But experiment with different combinations of loft and length to find the best driver for you.

Within this category, you have long irons (1 to 5), midirons (6 and 7), and short irons (8, 9, and wedges). Klippel suggests women carry no iron numbered lower than a 5-iron and instead load up on woods and wedges.

Wedges are basically short irons, and they go by name, not number. When buying wedges it's important to look at the loft each club has, expressed in degrees. The family of wedges, from longest wedge (lowest loft) to shortest, is *pitching wedge* (48 degrees), *gap wedge* (52 degrees), *sand wedge* (56 degrees), and *lob wedge* (60 degrees).

"To test different golf clubs before you buy, hit them! It's an outdoor activity. Stores should offer demo models for you to try. Make comparisons of three or four different models. Look for clubs that get balls airborne, feel solid, and take the effort out of the swing. Golf is all about the centeredness of the hit. What clubs give you this? If you have to struggle to make any of these happen, the club might not be right. Equipment should make the game easier. Trial and error is part of the process. Hit a longer club if you can. It will give you more distance if you can make centerface contact."

—Pat Lange, LPGA Master Professional and founder of Lange Golf, Golden, Colorado

Ideally there is a 10-yard gap between irons in the distance the ball travels, but players with slower swing speeds will notice more distance between their shorter irons than between their longer ones.

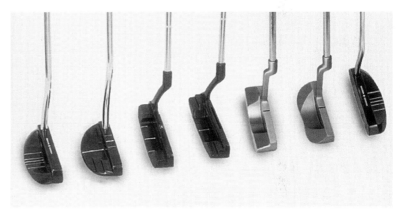

Putters come in many clubhead styles. Choose one that feels good and that appeals to your eye.

Putters

The two most important decisions you need to make when choosing a putter are its length and if it looks good to you. Most women play with putters that are too long—the standard unisex model sold is about 35 inches. For best results, look for a women's model or a unisex club that has a 33- or 34-inch shaft.

Notice the different head styles shown here. Don't fret about the names. Just try a few that appeal to you and see which one lets you roll the ball smoothly to the hole. And don't worry if you're fickle. Some golfers change putters in one season as often as they change socks.

BALLS, BAGS, AND ACCESSORIES

Golf balls

Each player needs her own ball and should have at least six balls for a round of golf (they get lost in the woods and the water). Buy them at any sporting goods store or golf course pro shop. There's a bewildering array of choices and some staggering prices. (Would you believe $45 a dozen?) Make

WHAT ARE WOMEN'S GOLF BALLS, ANYWAY?

● ● ● ● ● ● ● ● ● ● ● ● ● ● ● ● ● ● ●

A golf ball doesn't know if a man or a woman is hitting it, but you will find golf balls packaged as *women's*. All this really means is that the ball was designed to help players with slower swing speeds (and the industry likes to pigeon-hole all women in this cate-gory) get the ball up in the air more easily and maximize their distance. These balls typically have a harder cover and a larger core. There is an excel-lent variety of high-performing women's balls, and it makes life easier to buy these because then you don't have to sort through the techni-cal mumbo jumbo on the packaging of the dozens of other varieties. If you're a strong player there are balls designed to complement faster swing speeds, and these are unisex in their packaging. Finding a ball you like is mostly a matter of trial and error.

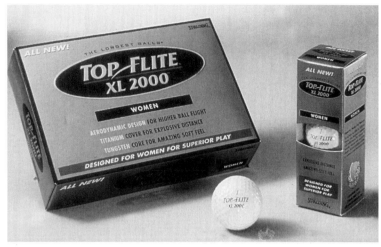

Pack plenty of golf balls (at least six per round), and look for women's balls, which are designed to complement slower swings.

your life easier to start by buying balls marked "for women." These balls have a large solid core designed to go farther. For a real bargain, check stores for "X-outs"—balls literally marked with Xs over the logo that didn't make the cut at the factory (mostly because of a minor cosmetic defect) but are still high performing.

Golf bags

You need a golf bag to carry your clubs, balls, tees, hat, water, snacks, wallet, and other sundries for the round. Lightweight and easy to carry (look for bags with a dou-ble shoulder strap) are my top priorities. Roomy, accessible pockets are nice too, so you can store a sweater or light jacket if you get warm during a round. For between rounds, your bag is like a closet, where you can stow your golf shoes, hat, golf glove, rain suit, and balls.

Bags fall into two basic categories: *lightweight carry bags* are for people who like to walk the course. Look for one with a

Bags with double shoulder straps are a welcome relief for your back.

Stand bags are lightweight and ideal for walking the course.

retractable metal stand, much like a bike's kickstand, so you can prop up your bag while you're hitting. *Cart bags* are bigger, more structured (harder), and heavier and are strapped onto the back of a golf cart. Some are light enough to carry. I have a *stand bag* that also easily straps onto the cart, so it's more versatile. Many bags are unisex, but women's bags are a bit shorter so that the shorter clubs don't disappear below the rim.

Some golf bags come with a detachable zippered pouch where you can stow your wallet, lip balm, jewelry, and other sundries for easy access and so you can take your valuables with you if leave your golf bag unattended.

Travel bag

Will you travel with your clubs? For airplane travel, you'll need a padded travel bag (akin to an oversize duffel) to protect your clubs. Get one with wheels to save your back as well.

Gloves

A golf glove is optional, but if you're blister prone, buy one. It will also prevent your hand from slipping on the grip in hot or

ATTENTION WOMEN SHOPPERS!

During my ten-plus years of selling golf equipment, I always gave women shoppers this advice: do your homework before pulling out your wallet and don't be intimidated when you walk into a golf store. Your money is worth as much as anybody else's, and you should receive the same service, time, and respect as any male customer would. If you don't like the attitude of the salespeople or don't trust them to sell you what you really need, go to a different store. Here are some other shopping tips.

- A lot of golf salespeople aren't at all educated about women's equipment but work under the assumption that all women are the same and thus should play with the same "ladies'" clubs.
- The salespeople at most off-course retailers work on commission and might be inclined to push you toward the brand they will make the most money on, even if it's not right for you.
- Don't let anyone rush you into buying something until you've fully researched several brands. There is no such thing as "must buy right now" when it comes to golf clubs; you will always be able to find similar deals on the same clubs somewhere else, even if a salesperson presents a now-or-never offer that sounds too good to pass up.
- Don't buy anything before testing it first. Find a facility that will lend you demos to hit, either into a net or, preferably, outside at a range. Once you've decided what brand to go with, make sure you get fitted. Your swing speed, hand size, and distance from wrist to floor should be measured to determine what shaft flex, grip size, and length you need in your clubs. If you're not offered this service, go somewhere else.
- Know that with most brand-name clubs, you don't have to buy the full set. You can start out with as few as you want and fill in the rest down the road.

—Stina Sternberg, equipment editor, *Golf For Women* magazine

rainy conditions. Right-handed golfers will buy a glove for the left hand and vice versa. More expensive gloves are made of cabretta leather, but there are some really good synthetics with wicking and quick-dry features. Gloves come in sizes small to extra large and in women's and men's models. How do you tell if the glove fits? Look for some flex or stretch through the knuckle area. It should be snug but not so tight that you can't comfortably make a fist or wiggle your fingers.

GLOVES

The pros use gloves everywhere on the course but the putting green, the theory being that without a glove you have more feel for delicate shots.

Towels

A golf towel—the size of a hand towel—is a necessity. Use it to wipe moisture, mud, and grass from your clubface and grips. Also, rest your club handle on the towel to prevent the grip from becoming soggy when the grass is wet. Some courses provide towels for the day, or you can buy one to hang from your bag (but then you have to wash it!).

Golf shoes

You can wear sneakers with grippy soles if you're just testing the waters, but if you're going to be golfing a lot buy some golf shoes, which are more to the purpose. Golf shoes have plastic spikes (or cleats) on the soles to provide traction and stability in the swing—both for performance and for safety, since wet grass is slippery. Look for waterproof or water-resistant models. Spikes wear down and fall out, so you should check your shoes regularly. To change a spike, buy a spike wrench and replacement spikes, available in golf shops, and simply twist them on and off.

Use a spike wrench (above) to change screw-in spikes every few months—more often if you're a golf junkie.

WHAT TO WEAR?

The dress code for golf courses, though relaxing somewhat, is fairly standard. You can't go wrong with a pair of khaki pants or walking shorts and a polo shirt. Some courses, particularly private clubs and tony resorts, have stricter dress codes (see page 86) that require collared shirts, but at most places women can be comfortable following this rule: if a top is sleeveless, it should have a collar. If it has sleeves, a crew or boat neck will do. Wherever you play, it's best to avoid tank tops, T-shirts, denim, and short shorts. Add a wide-brimmed hat, sunglasses, golf shoes, a light windbreaker or vest, depending on the weather, and you're ready to go.

WEATHER

In many parts of the country, golf is an all-weather, all-year sport, and you'll find yourself playing in rain, wind, and sun. Battling the elements may well enhance the challenge of the sport, but dressing the part is easy.

• •

POCKETS

Pockets are a golfer's best friend, so make sure your pants or shorts have roomy ones that can hold a golf ball or two and some tees.

• •

Sun

You'll be outside for about four hours in a typical round, so use the same sun sense you would under the same conditions anywhere else: bring a wide-brimmed hat or visor, sunglasses with UVA-UVB protection, and sunscreen. Look for a sunscreen with a quick-drying formula (gels and sprays are great) that won't leave your hands slimy. If it's beastly hot and sunny where you live, make an early morning or late afternoon tee time to avoid the burning hours of 10:00 A.M. to 3:00 P.M. If you're very fair-skinned you might want to consider a sun umbrella, which keeps you cooler and has a high sun-protection factor. (See chapter 10, Resources, for apparel companies that sell clothing with high SPF.)

Wind, rain, and cold

I don't particularly like playing in the rain—no matter what, glove, shoes, and grips will all get wet. But for added protection, keep a waterproof or water-resistant rain suit in the big pocket of your golf bag that you can pull out in a pinch. It's also not a bad idea to have an extra glove, an umbrella (most bags have a special slot for one), and a rain cover (a plastic hood that snaps onto your golf bag to keep your clubs dry). In cold and windy conditions, microfleece is great. And the manufacturer of your favorite golf glove probably carries winter golf gloves, too. Layer your clothing as you would for any outdoor activity, but make sure the protective outerwear is roomy enough in the arms and shoulders so you can swing freely.

Chapter 4

COURSE STUDIES

With any luck you've found a pro who's gotten you off the lesson tee and onto the golf course to help you start relating what you're learning to actually playing the game of golf.

WHAT IS GOLF?

Think *target sport*. It's a game where you hit a small, dimpled ball with a golf club over an outdoor playing field, the golf course. The standard course has eighteen holes. Each hole has a *teeing ground* or *tee*, where play begins for each hole, and a *fairway*, which connects the tee to the *green*, the velvety smooth surface where play for the hole ends. The goal for each hole is to get the ball in the *cup* (the hole in the green with the flagstick in it) from a set starting point (the *tee*) in as few strokes as possible.

"I find it is imperative that we get information regarding the distances from the forward tees before we make a tee time at a resort course. We have found some courses are really good designs for my husband but are absolutely insulting for me. We always check the distances from all the tee boxes before we reserve a tee time."

—Cheri Doege, golf nut

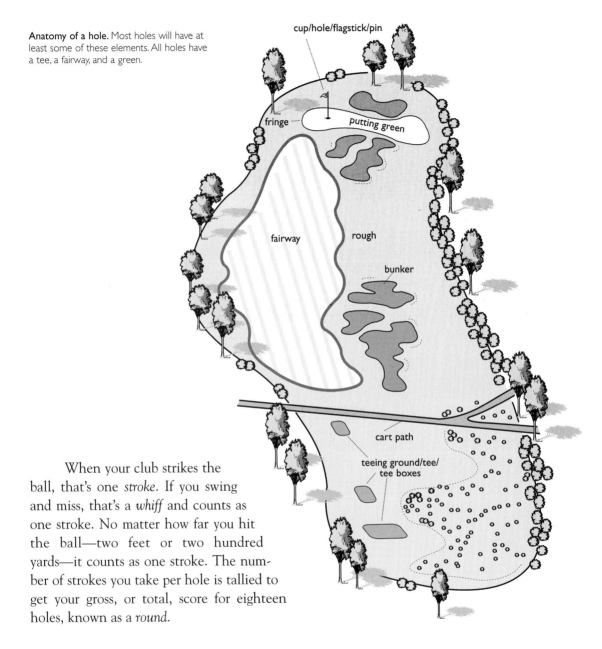

Anatomy of a hole. Most holes will have at least some of these elements. All holes have a tee, a fairway, and a green.

cup/hole/flagstick/pin

fringe

putting green

fairway

rough

bunker

cart path

teeing ground/tee/ tee boxes

When your club strikes the ball, that's one *stroke*. If you swing and miss, that's a *whiff* and counts as one stroke. No matter how far you hit the ball—two feet or two hundred yards—it counts as one stroke. The number of strokes you take per hole is tallied to get your gross, or total, score for eighteen holes, known as a *round*.

TOUR DE COURSE

You'll find courses in the desert, by the seaside, or in the mountains. No two golf courses are alike, varying in length, difficulty, and design. That's what makes the game so much fun. And I hope you won't become so obsessed with your score that you neglect to take in the scenery.

Despite the great variety among golf courses in landscape and terrain, all of them share the following features.

At the **teeing ground**, sets of tees are typically defined by the round colored markers. Distances to the green from each set are given on the scorecard.

Tee box

Teeing ground is the official term for the defined area where play starts on each hole, but most people call the area the *tee* or *tee box*. There are typically three to five tee boxes (also called *sets*

• •

"**C**hoosing what tees to play from is difficult for women. It can be a stretch on some courses to play from the middle tees, but playing from the forward tees means missing some design challenges from the tee box. For many years I played with men, and it was also awkward to be the only one rushing to hit from a different place. I simply started playing from the middle tees, and at some courses it meant that I was scoring higher than I knew I could."

—Amy DiAdamo, 20-something, avid golfer

TEE TIME

This one short word, *tee*, has several meanings in golf: at **tee time**,[1] place your ball on the **tee**[2] at the **tee**[3] to **tee off**.[4]

1. The time your group is scheduled to begin play at the first hole; the reservation made for play ("I'd like a tee time for Friday afternoon"). (See page 86).
2. The small wooden peg on which you balance your ball to play the first shot of each hole. It's not used elsewhere on the course.
3. The area from which you begin play on each hole.
4. To place the ball on the peg and begin play at a hole.

of tees) on each of the eighteen holes, and the line for each tee is clearly defined by a pair of colored markers (some look like oversize blocks or push pins). Each set of tees offers a different course length from tee to green, for different golfer abilities (see the scorecard on page 53). It's important to choose your tees according to your ability—as a new golfer you should start from the most forward set, which yields the shortest course. Play from the same set (color) of tees the entire round, using the colored makers as a guide.

Fairway

The *fairway* is also referred to as the *short grass*. This closely mown area that connects the tee and the green is where you want your tee shot to land, just as you hope the plane you're in lands on the runway. You might hear some fairways referred to as *doglegs*. This just means the fairway veers sharply to the left or right.

Rough

The *rough* is the longer, ragged grass that borders most fairways and greens. You don't want to be in the rough because you'll have less control over the distance and direction of your shot. But some players (I for one) don't mind being in short rough because the ball sits up nicely, almost as if it were teed up.

Fringe

The *fringe*, also known as the *collar* or *apron*, is an area of short grass (longer than the green and shorter than the rough) about two to three feet wide that encircles the green. It's a good spot to lay the flagstick while people are putting.

Above: This **fairway** is flanked by the cart path on the left and by water on the right. **Right:** The **fringe** creates a perimeter around the green.

Green

If you're feeling formal you may call the *green* the *putting surface*. Greens come in all shapes and sizes, but they all share one extremely important feature: the cup. The *cup* is a shallow metal cylinder 4¼ inches wide set into a hole in the green with a flagstick in it—the cup is where you want the ball to wind up. The terms *cup* and *hole* are interchangeable in this context, and the flagstick is also known as the *pin*. But *hole* is also used to mean the segment of the course from tee to green, as in "hole 6 is long."

Hazards

There are two types of *hazards*, or obstacles you don't want your ball to go into: *sand bunkers* and *water hazards*.

Bunkers are large sandy depressions that resemble an overgrown sandbox. You may hear them called *sand traps*, though most golf purists frown on the term. The ones farther from the green are known as *fairway bunkers*.

Red and yellow stakes mark water hazards such as ponds, wetlands, and other bodies of water; you'll usually incur penalty strokes (see chapter 8 on rules and etiquette for details) if your ball goes into a hazard. Sometimes spray-painted lines or fences take the place of the stakes.

Ball-washers are found near the tee box. To rid your ball of dirt and grass stains, lift the knob, insert the ball in the slot, pull up and push down vigorously a few times, and voilà! A clean golf ball.

- *Yellow* stakes denote *water hazards*, typically any body of water you have to hit your ball over—that is, that lies between your ball and its path to the green.

- *Red* stakes mark *lateral hazards*, most typically water, wetlands, or a ditch that runs parallel to the fairway.

Out-of-bounds

Out-of-bounds refers to the area outside the boundaries of the course. *White* stakes mark the *boundary line* of the golf course. You must replay any ball that lands out-of-bounds, also called OB.

Types of golf courses

There are four basic types of golf courses, which vary in length and difficulty. As a new golfer, seek out smaller ones.

Eighteen-hole regulation courses. This is the gold standard. Here's what it means:

"**S**ome of the long par 4s I can never reach in two shots. So I practice my short iron shots more than anything else. I need to work more on my putting in order to get those pars."

—Lucretia Bingham, forty-year player, handicap "somewhere around 20"

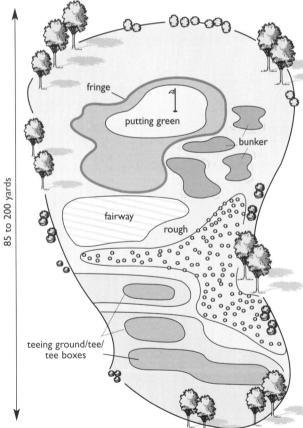

fringe

putting green

bunker

fairway

rough

teeing ground/tee/ tee boxes

85 to 200 yards

A par 3.

eighteen holes, par 71 to 74, a mix of par-3, -4, and -5 holes. The course length can range from about 4,800 yards from the forward tees to about 7,000 yards from the back tees. You can establish a handicap playing on these courses.

Nine-hole courses. Just what they sound like. As long as the golf course has a USGA slope and course rating, you may post a score for handicap purposes.

Par-3 courses. These are a great choice for new golfers. Whether it's a nine-hole course or the more standard eighteen, all the holes are par 3s, which means they're approximately 85 to 200 yards. Par is 54. You cannot post a score from a par-3 course for handicap purposes.

Executive courses. Many people confuse these with par 3s. An executive course is nine or eighteen holes and a mix of par 3s, 4s, and 5s. It is significantly shorter than a standard eighteen-hole course, with a par of 60 to 68. Because it's shorter it's a good choice for new players or those who don't want to spend four or five hours playing golf.

SCORING

Understanding par

Each golf hole is marked as either a *par 3*, *par 4*, or *par 5*. An eighteen-hole course uses a combination of these three types of holes to comprise a standard course of par 72.

The "par" assigned to a given hole is the standard number of strokes a scratch golfer (one who shoots par) would take to get the ball from the tee into the cup. Pars are generally determined by how long the hole is; par 3s are the shortest holes. For example:

- On a par 3, the scratch golfer should take one shot to get to the green and two putts to get the ball in the hole. This is three strokes, which is par for the hole.

- On a par 4, two shots to get to the green and two putts equals four strokes.

- On a par 5, three shots to get to the green with two putts equals five strokes.

If you play the hole according to the guidelines above, you are said to have played the hole *in regulation*. When you choose what set of tees you are playing from, choose the set whose yardage gives you the best chance to play the hole in regulation. That said, you can still make par if you don't play the hole to the letter—and most people don't. Say on a par 3 you take two shots to get on the green and one stroke to sink the putt. That's three strokes and a par.

All scoring terms are defined in relation to par.

- **Par.** A score equal to par; for example, a 4 on a par 4. People who shoot par consistently over eighteen holes are called *scratch golfers*.

- **Birdie.** One under par on a hole.

- **Bogey.** One stroke over par on a hole. There are also double (two over par), triple, and quadruple bogeys, and so on. You may hear people refer to themselves as *bogey golfers*. That's someone who shoots about 90.

- **Eagle.** Two strokes under par on a hole. As rare as a bald eagle.

- **Hole-in-one** or **ace.** The ball goes from the tee into the cup in one stroke. If you get one, consider yourself extremely lucky and buy all your friends iced tea to celebrate. Better yet, tell *Golf For Women* magazine about it, and the editors will send you a hole-in-one tag for you to hang proudly on your golf bag.

• •

"**O**ne avid friend of mine has been hacking her way around her club for several years, loving the game but feeling miserably nonathletic. Her defining moment came when she played alone, hooked up with three old duffers by the starter. From 160 yards out, she jammed herself down over the ball and slammed it to within three feet of the pin. She nailed her birdie putt. The duffers thought she was a star. She had triple bogeys on the next two holes but it didn't matter. In her mind she'd become a player."

—Lucretia Bingham

• •

PARS ARE FOR PROS

• •

It's ludicrous and self-defeating for most players, particularly new golfers, to compare themselves with par. The average player in the United States shoots 100, which is about 28 strokes over par.

For a confidence boost, set a *personal par*, a par for the hole or course that is realistic and attainable based on your skill level (of course this practice is not allowed in a competition).

My mother, for example, would always convert a par 5 into a par 6 in her mind if she knew there was no way she'd reach the green in regulation (three shots) even with her most brilliant efforts. Teaching pro Dede Braun of Golf Divas recommends that her newer players add two strokes to every hole so their par on a par-72 course would be 108.

Here's another confidence-boosting scoring system, devised for new players by the LPGA Teaching and Club Professional division: Refer to your scorecard to find out what the par is on the hole you're about to play. For example, if you're playing a par 3, you have three strokes to get the ball on the green (four on a par 4 and so on). If you are not on in three, pick up the ball and place it within ten yards of the green and play in from that point. Take up to three strokes from that spot (or whatever the official par is for the hole) to get the ball in the cup; move on to the next hole at that point even if you haven't sunk your putt.

Reading and marking a scorecard

Your scorecard is a pocket map of the golf course, full of helpful directional information. Be sure to read it before you get out on the course so you know what to expect. Here's a user-friendly guide to understanding one.

The card at right reflects how eighteen-hole courses are divided into two nines: the *front nine*, holes one through nine, and the *back nine*, ten through eighteen. (This example shows you how to keep score for *stroke*, or *medal*, *play*, where every shot must be counted. For details on how to mark a scorecard for *match play*, which is a hole-by-hole competition, and other games, see chapter 9, Have Fun!)

A. Hole and course **yardages** are given from the tee to the green for each of the five sets of tees, which are distinguished by color: green, white, blue, black, and stone. (On some golf courses the tees are given names such as *forward, middle, championship.*) For example, hole 7 is 449 yards from the green tees. The scorecard also totals the yardage for the front nine ("Out"), the back nine ("In"), and finally indicates the total yardage for all eighteen holes for each set of tees ("Tot").

Look at the scorecard yardages before you play to determine which set of tees you should play from (see Do I Have to Play from the Forward Tees? sidebar, page 54). On this scorecard, the italic numbers after the tee color give the recommended handicap range for that set of tees.

	Hole / Men/Women	1	2	3	4	5	6	7	8	9	OUT	P L A Y E R	10	11	12	13	14	15	16	17	18	IN	TOT	HCP	NET
Stone	Permission Only	426	435	227	383	546	194	573	462	448	3694		436	163	412	557	200	360	467	427	563	3585	7279		
Black	0-6	399	412	208	354	532	180	542	437	430	3494		406	148	373	531	179	334	441	409	540	3361	6855		
Blue	7-15 / 0-4	381	393	181	343	519	157	529	416	407	3326		375	137	349	521	154	311	416	390	527	3180	6506		
White	16-26 / 5-14	371	353	167	309	497	147	508	389	329	3070		356	123	315	484	133	302	384	324	496	2917	5987		
Green	27+ / 15+	342	328	146	257	434	125	449	373	257	2711		307	96	265	436	118	220	310	283	373	2408	5119		
Molly		6	5	4	4	8	4	6	5	6	48		7	4	5	6	5	6	7	3	7	50	98	28	70
Grace		5	5	3	5	6	4	8	5	5	46		5	4	5	6	4	5	5	5	6	45	91	20	71
PAR		4	4	3	4	5	3	5	4	4	36		4	3	4	5	3	4	4	4	5	36	72		
HANDICAP		7	3	9	17	13	15	11	5	1			8	18	4	14	12	16	2	6	10				
DATE		SCORER										ATTESTED BY								TEES					

Recommended Tees — C — D E F G

A scorecard filled in according to **stroke play** scoring. In stroke play, you keep track of every stroke you take during a round. After each player's course handicap is subtracted from her total score, the player with the lowest net score wins.

B. The **Par** row indicates the designated par score for each of the eighteen holes—par 3, 4, or 5—and will give you the total par for the course. Here it is 72.

C. The **Out** box in the Out column is where each player notes her total score for the first nine holes. In this round, Molly shot a 48. She's 12 strokes over par on the first nine holes.

D. The **In** box in the In column is where each player notes her total score for the back nine, the second nine holes. Molly shot 50 on the back nine.

E. The **Total** score is also known as your gross score; this is the number of strokes each player took to play eighteen holes before she adjusted her score based on her course handicap. Molly shot a 98. (Handicaps are explained in the section below.)

F. The **Handicap** box ("HCP") is where each player writes her course handicap. Molly's is a 28.

G. The **Net** box contains *net* score, which is the total (gross) score minus the handicap for each player. Molly's gross score is 98. Her handicap is 28, so she subtracts 28 from 98 to yield a net score of 70. This net score beats her opponent Grace's net score of 71.

H. The **Handicap** row ranks the eighteen holes by difficulty, with 1 generally being the most difficult and 18 the easiest. If you aren't playing against someone, don't worry about this line. It's used as a guide to where you receive strokes in competition. See chapter 9.

I. The **Date**, **Scorer**, and **Attest** areas record the data for the round. Technically, one member of your group is the official marker, or scorekeeper. He or she should sign the card at the end of the round. Another member of your group should attest the score.

DO I HAVE TO PLAY FROM THE FORWARD TEES?

Signs at the tee box give you the yardage to the green for each of the sets of tees.

You've probably heard the red or most forward tees referred to as the *women's tees*. Erase this backward thought from your mind right now! On older courses, where there were often only three tees, the color for the forward tees was always red. The middle set was white, and the farthest back was blue. Hence the red tees became known as the "ladies' tees" because most women played from them. There is no rule stating either that forward tees must be red or that women must play from them. In fact most new courses are very good about avoiding this color assignment.

All golfers, men and women, should play from the set that suits their skill level. See the scorecard on page 53 and note at the description of A on page 52 that it recommends tees to play based on handicap, not gender. This is progress. I play from the forward tees because I'm not a long hitter. My average drives are about 160 to 170 yards. Most new golfers and juniors should play from these tees. My friends Heidi and Stina, who can hit their drives more than 200 yards, play from farther back. Forward tee yardages vary widely among courses. Start paying attention to the scorecard yardage and you'll find out what course length, and therefore which set of tees, you should play from. For new golfers, a course length of 4,800 to 5,200 yards is ideal. Experiment, and remember—if you can crush the ball, it's OK not to play from the forward tees!

HANDICAPS SIMPLIFIED

What is a handicap?

A *handicap* is an artificial numerical advantage or disadvantage (an allotment of strokes) given to golfers to equalize competition. Handicaps are determined following USGA guidelines and under USGA oversight (see the How Do I Get a Handicap? section, pages 57–58).

The beauty and purpose of the handicap system is that it levels the playing field, enabling golfers of different abilities to compete against one another. The lower your handicap, the better you are. Let's go back to

HANDICAP HOW-TOS

Scorecards have two sets of numbers that baffle many a player: *course rating* and *slope*.

- **Course rating** is the figure assigned to each set of tees to indicate the course's overall playing difficulty for a scratch golfer. It is based on yardage, hazards, width of fairways, and other such factors that may affect a player's scoring ability.
- **Slope** indicates an average golfer's potential scoring ability on the course. The lowest slope is 55 (an easy course) and the highest is 155 (very hard). A golf course of standard playing difficulty, as defined by the USGA, has a slope of 113.

Men's	Course Rating	Slope
Blue	72.3	135
White	70.2	130
Gold	66.1	117

Women's	Course Rating	Slope
White	75.7	131
Gold	70.6	120
Red	68.2	111

The men's and women's USGA **course rating** and **slope** from each set of tees will be printed somewhere on the scorecard. The numbers and your eighteen-hole score will be used to update or establish your handicap index.

Don't worry about the technical mumbo jumbo behind these figures. You need pay attention only to what these numbers are for two handicap purposes:

- **Posting a score.** Let's say you played from the gold tees. To establish your handicap index—which is based on the ten best scores out of the twenty most recent ones—you would *post*, or record, the following numbers after your round: your gross score, the course rating (70.6), and the slope for the tees you played (120). Most courses have a computer in the pro shop where you input these numbers. Your index is updated every two weeks in season.
- **Determining your course handicap.** Once you have an index, you must convert it to determine your course handicap, the number of strokes allotted to you for the particular course you are playing.
  The slope is used to convert your index to a course handicap. Most golf courses post a Course Handicap Table that lists what your course handicap is based on your index and on the tees you are playing. Or you can do the math yourself by multiplying your index by the quotient of the slope divided by 113. For example, your index is 26.4 and you're playing from the gold tees, which have a slope of 120. Your course handicap is 28 (26.4 × 120 ÷ 113).
  To tell the truth, I don't know anyone who does this for casual rounds—most people just estimate—but if you're in a tournament you must do the math.

Ideally, all sets of tees should have ratings for both men and women, but many courses—wrongly assuming that all women play from the forward tees—don't rate them all for women. If you encounter this situation, ask the head pro at the course how you should proceed if you want to post the score.

Play from the set of tees appropriate for your skill level. For new golfers, that's the forward tees.

that scorecard on page 53 to see what I mean. Grace's gross score was 91. That beats Molly's gross score of 98. However, once these scores are adjusted using each player's course handicap, Molly, the higher handicapper, comes out the winner. Subtract her 28 handicap from 98 and she gets a net 70, one stroke lower than Grace's net 71 (subtracting her handicap of 20).

You can look at your handicap as the average number of strokes over par you will shoot on a standard par 72 course, though the USGA does not sanction this view because golf courses vary in length, difficulty, and par. In a basic, nontechnical example, let's say your handicap at your par-72 home course is 20—on a good day you could shoot 92. If you play at an easier course, you are expected to shoot a better score, say an 89, and your course handicap for that round should reflect this advantage and be lower, say 18.

"I had lessons and dabbled as a child but didn't start playing seriously until about five years ago, at age 24. I play about once or twice a month. My handicap index is still 40 (ugh!). When I'm playing a lot I shoot around 105."

—Tara Gravel, associate editor, *Golf Magazine*

• •

AVERAGE HANDICAP INDEX

The highest handicap index for women is 40.4, though your course handicap can be higher, up to 44. The average handicap index for women registered with the USGA system is 30.1. Try not to get hung up on what your handicap index is, but make sure it honestly reflects how you play. It can serve as a good measure of your progress.

• •

Because courses with the same par vary in difficulty, the USGA Handicap System establishes two numbers for every golfer: a handicap index and a course handicap.

A *handicap index* indicates a player's potential scoring ability; when golfers refer to their handicap, they are technically referring to their handicap index. Your index is based on the ten best scores out of your twenty most recent ones, and it is updated every two weeks in season.

A *course handicap* is the number of strokes allotted to you for the particular course you are playing that day, based on its relative difficulty. You use your index and the *slope* of the tees you are playing from to determine your course handicap. See the Handicap How-Tos sidebar for the formula used to convert your index to a course handicap.

How do I get a handicap?

To obtain a handicap index, see if the course you regularly play offers a handicap tracking service (private clubs do, and most public courses do, as well). You'll be charged a small fee. If it doesn't, contact the USGA for a listing of state and regional golf associations that provide the service.

After a round of golf, you submit your gross score (total number of strokes) plus the slope and rating of the course you just played. A computer uses these three numbers to calculate your handicap index, a numeral expressed in decimals—26.4, for example. Once you have a handicap index, you can get a course handicap for any course that has an official USGA slope and course rating. Let's say you're invited to play in a member-guest tournament. The pro will ask for your index so she can figure what your course handicap for the event is.

If you have a casual golf outing coming up and you don't yet have a handicap index, you can compute an unofficial course handicap yourself. Take the average of your past five scores and subtract from that average the par for the course you will play. For example, your last five rounds were 100, 105, 103, 102, and 95, for an average of 101. Subtract 72 (par) to come up with 29, your course handicap.

The truth is that a lot of golfers don't keep handicaps. I didn't have one for years. And most

You'll find golf courses in the woods, the mountains, the desert—almost anywhere, in fact.

people estimate. That's the reality. You can play just fine without one. Don't fret unless you're joining a serious competitive league.

If you're planning to get serious about the game and want to establish a handicap index, for the complete official story visit the USGA's Web site (www.usga.org).

P.S. If all of the above still reads like Greek to you, rest assured it will make more sense once you gain some playing experience.

Chapter 5

IT'S SWING TIME

I'm not a golf instructor, though I work with some of the best instructors in the business to present the fundamentals of the golf swing, in simplest terms, to readers of *Golf for Women* magazine. Some teachers are very technical, describing precise positions students should strive for. Other coaches focus more on the feel and rhythm of the swing. That focus is the goal in this chapter, and it's why Krista Dunton, an LPGA and PGA teaching professional at Forsgate Country Club in Jamesburg, New Jersey, will be our coach. Dunton, who works with lots of women as well as new golfers, has a simple teaching philosophy: Feel. Trust. Swing.

"My secret to success? I've worked very, very hard at my game and have been very determined to get to this position. And most importantly, I've worked with one coach all my life and have just kept things very simple and not made golf too complicated."

—Karrie Webb, LPGA Tour professional

Without getting into much technical jargon, she'll show us how to prepare properly for hitting the ball, which is half the battle in making a good swing! Here's what Dunton has to say.

Practice mimicking the swing positions of LPGA Tour pro Grace Park.

WATCH THE SWING

I always show my students what a model swing looks like so they can see what they're trying to accomplish. Rather than watching friends on the golf course, who might not have perfected their own swings, watch the LPGA tournaments on television, where you'll see the best swings.

Here is LPGA Tour professional Grace Park in motion. A rookie in 2000, Park is one of the longest hitters on the tour. Stand in front of a mirror and mimic her positions. (Park is extremely flexible, so don't strain yourself to turn your shoulders as far as she does.) Observe the swing. Imitate it. That's how children learn, and you'll lose this ability if you get caught up in the technical hows and whys.

1. **Setup.** Park has a balanced setup, with her weight distributed equally between her feet. Her upper body is tilted slightly to the right; this will help her stay behind the ball while her momentum is going through impact.

2. **Takeaway.** Her shoulders, arms, hands, and club start the backswing together in a one-piece takeaway while her lower body remains quiet. The triangle her arms and club form stays together as she takes the club away. The shaft is in line with her toes and parallel to the ground, with the toe of the club pointing to the sky.

3. **Top of the backswing.** Minimal hip rotation and a big shoulder turn help to create power. Park's weight is on the inside of her right leg—your weight goes in the direction the club is swinging and should always remain centered between your feet. Notice how she maintains the knee flex she had at setup.

4. **Impact.** Notice how her upper body and head stay behind the ball through impact. The club and her left arm form a straight line.

5. **Follow-through.** Notice the full extension of her arms down the target line after impact, and her right hand and forearm have rotated over her left.

6. **Finish.** She finishes in a balanced position, and her weight has fully shifted to her left side. Her belt buckle is facing the target, as are her right shoelaces.

> •
>
> Instructions here are for right-handed players; reverse if you're left-handed.
>
> •

LEARN YOUR SETUP ABCs

There are so many variables in golf—the weather, the course conditions, your mood—so don't make your setup one of them. The setup writes the script for a successful swing. Set up poorly and you'll hit a bad shot. Set up well and you have the best chance to make a good swing and repeat it. If something goes wrong in your swing, check your setup. It may take only a minor adjustment to get you back on track.

Guarantee a good grip

A common mistake among women is to place the club too much in the palms. To get the feeling of a good grip, pick up a suitcase or hammer. See how the handle rests more in your fingers than your palm? The golf club should do the same. Think of these two images when you put your left hand (right hand for left-handed players) on the top of the grip. With the handle toward the base of the fingers of your left hand your wrists, a source of power, can freely hinge and unhinge in the swing, just as they do when you hammer a nail.

Pick up a suitcase with your left hand. See how the handle rests at the base of your fingers. Grip the club the same way with your left hand.

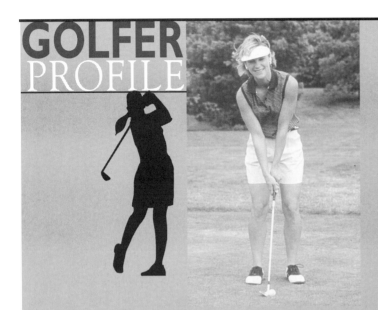

GOLFER PROFILE

KRISTA DUNTON

Director of Instruction,
    Forsgate Country Club,
    Jamesburg, New Jersey
Started golfing: age 9
Age: 34
College golf:
    University of Michigan
Professional golf:
    played 4 years on
    the Futures Tour

WHAT DO YOU LOVE MOST ABOUT THE GAME?

Playing with my mom in the evening on cool summer nights when I was a kid is how I first got exposed to golf and where my fondest memories of the game still lie. I love golf because it's one of the most challenging physical and mental games you'll ever play. You're never quite satisfied with your performance, which makes you constantly strive to improve. You learn more about yourself and how you react to pressure than in any other game. There's no one to blame; it's a test between you and the course. I love the way golf is a different game every time you go out to play. Each course is shaped by and carved into its natural environment. Playing in the desert or the mountains or the northern woods is unique in each case. I love to walk the course so I can take in the entire experience of being outdoors and enjoy the peacefulness of the game.

WHAT'S THE BIGGEST CHALLENGE IN TEACHING GOLF?

People don't fully realize how much time and patience golf takes. It parallels life in so many ways. In order to improve, you need to practice and play as much as possible. It's a game that evolves over time. I always tell people it's a lifetime sport: not only is it one of the few sports you can play for a lifetime, but it takes about that much time to figure it all out!

Convincing people to hang in there during the tough times and to trust themselves on the golf course is challenging. With all the high-tech gear, everyone expects results so quickly. This game is not like that. You need to work hard, practice as much as you can, and stay committed through bad times and good times.

IS THERE A DIFFERENCE BETWEEN TEACHING MEN AND TEACHING WOMEN?

I hate to generalize since there are always exceptions, but women tend to be more open to instruction because they have less tendency to want to do it "their way." The athletic ego is not as pronounced in women as in men. However, that also makes teaching men easier at times because they trust their athletic instincts more than women do. The best students are athletic women with good hand-eye coordination who take instruction well.

WHAT'S THE BIGGEST CHALLENGE IN PLAYING GOLF? ◄----------------

Learning to trust yourself and not try to "fix" your swing every time you hit a bad shot is a huge challenge. In each round you play you will hit good shots and bad shots, lucky shots and unlucky shots. The key is to stay patient and positive and not let the perfectionist in you get in the way of playing a good round. Develop a routine you can rely on, stay focused on your target, and trust your swing. Golf is a humbling game at all skill levels, and you need to stay confident, almost arrogant, so that you totally believe in your ability and there is little self-doubt.

WHAT ARE THE MOST IMPORTANT THINGS A GOLFER CAN DO TO IMPROVE?

Find a good teaching professional you relate to well. Practice and play as often as you can, but spend your time on the practicing range and playing golf on the course. Learn about your swing and the parts that are important to you. Don't listen to every piece of advice; stay specific to your game and your swing. What works for one does not work for all. Practice just as hard on your short game as on your full swing. Compete as often as possible, even if it's just a friendly match for a soft drink. Playing with something on the line will teach you to focus. Also, stay in good physical shape. For women, strong shoulders, abdomen, hands, and arms are key.

Also, be receptive to change. All athletes go through making changes in their technique when learning a sport, and golf is certainly no different. Many times women don't improve simply because they resist change. Perhaps it's uncomfortable or results aren't immediate, but all changes take some time.

HOW DO YOU ENCOURAGE WOMEN TO STAY WITH THE GAME?   ◄----------------

Time is the toughest issue with women because they always have so much going on in their lives. Go out and play nine holes late in the day when you're not taking up such a big chunk of time. Let golf be the time for you to relax, to let out stress, to get exercise, to build friendships, and to enjoy a great game!

Find friends who love to play, or join a league or a club to meet new people who play. Golfers are passionate and love to share the game with others, so it's never hard to find people with a similar interest.

I'd like to acknowledge the four most influential people in my teaching life. Tim Baldwin, former women's golf coach at Stanford University, taught me how to play. Mike Adams, director of instruction at PGA National, taught me how to teach. The love and support of my parents have been essential. My mom taught swimming and tennis for most of her life. My dad was the pitching coach for the Stanford University baseball team, and he developed some champion athletes. My parents gave me the skills to communicate my thoughts effectively and taught me to chase my dreams with hard work and passion. —K.D.

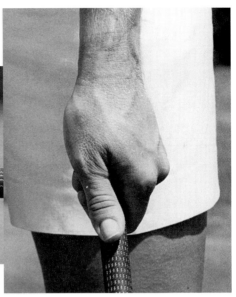

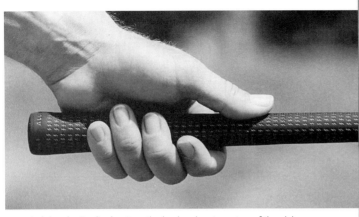

Left-hand grip checkpoints: the heel pad rests on top of the club; you can see two to three knuckles of your left hand.

Your left hand. The key to a good grip is in your left-hand position (above right). Position the top hand as if you were holding that suitcase or hammer so that

- the grip handle runs diagonally across the fingers and the top of the palm so that the heel pad of your left hand sits on top of the club

- two to three knuckles are visible

- the left thumb is just right of the center of the grip handle

Your right hand. When placing your right hand on the grip, your goal is to join the hands so they can work as a unit. Check that

- the V formed by the thumb and forefinger is closed (there's no gap)

- the right palm faces the target, not the sky or the ground

- the club handle runs diagonally across the fingertips (between the top and middle joints)

Right-hand grip checkpoints. Join the hands so they work as a unit. Extend the index finger down the shaft. It should run parallel to the handle. Return to the ready position by curling your finger back under the club.

There are three ways of joining your hands on the club. Go with the one that's most comfortable and that best unites your hands.

Ten-finger (baseball) grip. Krista likes to start new golfers, juniors, and women with this grip. All your fingers are on the handle, providing good control, strength, and speed. This works well for individuals with small hands.

Overlap grip. Your right pinkie rests on top of your left index finger. This is the most widely used grip and is good for players with medium or large hands and long fingers.

Interlock grip. Your right pinkie snuggles between the base of your left index and middle fingers, interlocking with the index finger. This works well for people with thin, small fingers and small to medium-sized hands.

Grip pressure. Most new players grip the club too tightly, which will inhibit the clubhead speed you can generate and negatively influence the direction of the ball. Think of holding a pen; you want enough pressure to control the pen but not so much that your handwriting is choppy.

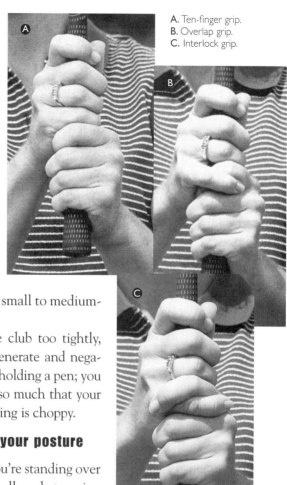

A. Ten-finger grip.
B. Overlap grip.
C. Interlock grip.

Perfect your posture

When you're standing over the golf ball ready to swing (this is called the *address* position), your body is in an athletic "ready" position. Your weight is centered and balanced on the balls of your feet, which are hip-width to shoulder-width apart, depending on the club you're hitting. As your clubs get shorter your stance gets narrower.

Your arms hang naturally and the upper body is free of tension. Throw vanity to the wind and stick your rear end out and up. Add a small amount of knee flex, keeping your knees in line with your ankles, and you're set to

Set up with your feet about shoulder-width apart; narrow your stance slightly when hitting short irons

Here's a foolproof way to set up for success taught to Krista by Mike Adams of PGA National. Standing tall with your back straight (no slouching) and knees slightly flexed, place your hands on your thighs. Bend forward from your hips until your fingertips touch the tops of your knees. Let your arms dangle and grab a club. You're ready to swing.

go. When you're in a good posture you'll feel some tightness on the insides of your legs down to your ankles. Since your right hand is lower on the club, the right shoulder is naturally lower than the left shoulder. This puts your upper body at a slight tilt to the right, which will help you keep your head behind the ball through impact. Many players incorrectly level their shoulders at address.

Determine ball position

The distance you stand from the ball increases as your clubs get longer, but you should never reach for the ball (see photo page 67). Keep your upper arms, from the elbows up, against your chest. As a rule, there should be about a hand's width of space between your club handle and your thighs.

When determining where to play the ball in your stance—closer to your left foot or right foot, go by what club you're hitting. Ball position starts in the middle of your stance with the short irons and inches forward as the clubs get longer (see photo page 67). Krista also teaches

"**T**hanks to my past life as a touring pro, I'm obsessed with giving women more distance on their tee shots. Ninety percent of my students want those extra yards, and I want them to have them. Therefore, if I could give but one tip to women it would be to set up with your heels apart at least the distance of your hips, not your shoulders. Unlike the typical male, with shoulders wider than hips, many women have narrow shoulders and wider hips. So let your hips be your guide and take a wider stance. The stable platform will help you swing through the ball and let her rip! As I like to say, 'Hip, hip, hurray!' "

—Debbie Steinbach, LPGA professional, The Reserve, Indian Wells, California

her students to use their upper bodies as a reference point for positioning the ball.

- With your wedges and mid- to short irons, line up the ball off the left side of your face.

- Fairway woods and long irons are played about one ball width forward of that, toward your left foot. Use the logo of your shirt as a guideline.

- The ball position for the driver and teed-up woods is just inside your left heel, or lined up with the left armpit.

No matter what club you're hitting, make sure you set up with your head behind the ball. If your head and upper body are ahead of the ball at address, you'll increase your chances of muffing your shot.

Take aim

None of the advice above matters much if you don't have a target in mind. You must determine exactly where you want your ball to go and aim there. The more specific and narrow your target, the better. Think of an archer who aims at the bull's-eye, not the entire target circle.

Ball position gets closer to your front foot as the clubs you're hitting get longer.

To take aim, go back to geometry class and think parallel lines. A classic image is a set of railroad tracks running from the ball and your body to the target. The outer track, where the ball sits, is the *target line* (the white tubes in the photo on the following page represent the railroad tracks). This is the imaginary line on which you aim your clubface squarely at your target. "Squarely" simply means that the clubface is perpendicular to the target line. The inner railroad track is where you align your feet, knees, hips, shoulders, and eyes so they're parallel to the target line.

"**S**tay visual. Visualize the flight of the ball and see it going to the target. See yourself making the swing that will do the job of getting the ball to where you want it to go. If you can see it, you can do it!"

—Krista Dunton

Right: Use the simple visual image of a clockface to help you aim the clubface squarely at your target. The club's leading (bottom) edge is aligned so that the toe of the edge is at 12:00 and the heel is at 6:00. Many golfers make the mistake of aligning the top edge of the clubhead, which tends to close the clubface. **Below:** Align your feet, knees, hips, and shoulders so they are parallel to your target line.

target line

Here's a quick tip to make sure you're aimed properly. Aim the clubface toward the target and visualize a line going from the clubface to the target. Turn your head slightly to the left and let your eyes look down that line to the target. If you're not lined up correctly, you'll be looking either left or right of your target.

It will help if you perform this aiming routine before every shot.

1.   Pick your target from behind the ball; you'll have a truer perspective than when you line up standing over the ball.

2.   Always aim your clubface at your target before you set up to the ball. Remember, it should be perpendicular (square) to the imaginary target line (the outer railroad track). To help ensure that the clubface is aimed correctly, pick an intermediate target—say, a patch of grass or a spot—a few inches in front of your ball on the target line.

3.   Then align your body so that the lines of your feet, knees, hips, and shoulders are parallel to it and the target line. Think of those railroad tracks. Always build your setup around the clubface. Once you're set up, take one last look at your target and fire away.

GET IN FULL SWING

Once you're set up well over the ball, your swing should take care of itself—in theory, at least. Here are just a few thoughts to keep you going in the right direction, and don't forget to refer to Grace Park's swing sequence.

●   Stay loose. To play golf well, you need to be as loose as a noodle, relaxed and tension-free. Tension in the arms and upper body robs you of distance. Think soft arms and hands.

Left: Turn your left shoulder over your right knee to maximize your power potential. **Below:** Key checkpoint: your left arm and club should form an *L*.

- Learn to turn. A good shoulder turn is the key to power, so get that left shoulder over your right knee at the top of your backswing. Also, use your chin as a checkpoint. In the backswing the left shoulder brushes the chin. In the forward swing, the right shoulder brushes the chin.

- Watch your weight. Just as in skiing, your weight needs to stay between your feet; never allow it to sway to the outside. Your shoulders stay stacked over your hips.

- Get your arms swinging. As your left arm swings across your chest, the right arm folds and the wrists naturally hinge. Your hands and arms stay in front of your body throughout the swing.

- Stay in your posture. You don't want to stand up as you swing or lunge toward the ball. Maintain the posture and knee flex you established in your setup through impact. It might help to envision keeping the crease in your pants that forms at the top of your thigh. If you stand up, you'll lose the crease.

- Create resistance. You're coiling the upper body around a stable lower body to create some tension and resistance—think of it as stored energy—that you unleash in the downswing. Coil into your right hip and unwind into your left hip.

- Start your downswing from the ground up. Many players incorrectly start with the upper body, throwing the club at the ball.

GETTING THE BALL AIRBORNE

• • • • • • • • • • • • • • • • • • • •

Here's a three-step drill Krista loves that will have you hitting balls before you know it. Grab a 7-iron and go.

1. Start by swinging the club halfway back and halfway through so it brushes the grass.

2. Put a tee in the grass, pushed about halfway in, and swing the club so it clips the tee out of the ground and into the air.

3. Tee up a ball and take smooth half swings, again knocking the tee out of the ground. The ball will go up in the air.

Maintain your posture and some right knee flex in your backswing.

• Create some rhythm in your swing. Say to yourself as you swing, "Back-2-3; down-2-3." Feel the same pace back and through.

• Finish strong. Make a nice full follow-through so your belt buckle faces the target. Your weight should be completely on your left side when you finish the swing, with your right toe pointed like a ballerina's.

You might hear the term **swing plane**, which simply refers to the arc the club takes around your body as you swing it back and through. An ideal swing plane is not straight up and down, nor is it horizontal; it's somewhere between, as shown here.

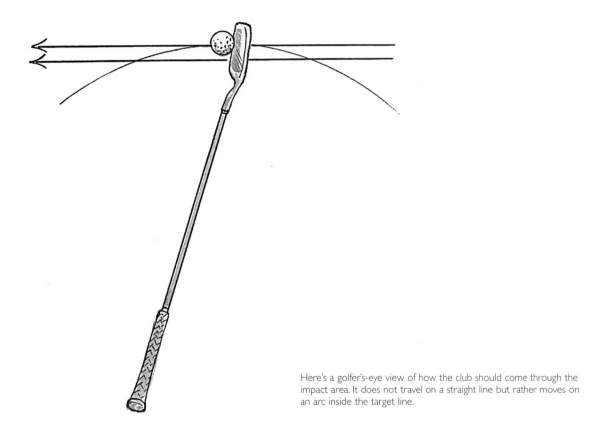

Here's a golfer's-eye view of how the club should come through the impact area. It does not travel on a straight line but rather moves on an arc inside the target line.

IGNORE THESE SWING THOUGHTS

It's amazing how often Krista hears golfers offer this advice: "Keep your head down and your left arm straight." It's become the rallying cry of poor instruction, mostly from well-meaning but ill-informed men. Without going into a lengthy treatise, here's why you should ignore this advice.

Keep your head down. Many golfers translate this to mean your head should stay fixed over the ball. If you keep your head stationary you'll do a classic reverse pivot, where your weight stays on your left side in your backswing. Your head is attached to

"**M**ost women need to build speed in their swings, which will give them more distance. Very few people swing too fast. It's just that the speed might be in the wrong spot in their swing— like at the start of the downswing. Keep the speed at the bottom of the swing, swinging with acceleration and balance."

—Krista Dunton

HELP! A BIG PART OF MY SWING STRUGGLE IS MY LARGE BUST

• • • • • • • • • • • • • • • • •

"I'm a three-year beginner with a 42-inch bust and have taken lessons with male instructors off and on. Most of them don't know what to do with female students with an ample bosom. Frankly, they're too embarrassed to go there in a teaching session."

That's definitely a valid question, and if you're well endowed you'll need to adjust your setup slightly. You need room to swing the club, so take a big bend from the hips and place both arms more on top of your chest, rather than to the side.

your shoulders, so allow it to move laterally a bit when you make your shoulder turn, but do keep your eyes focused on the back of the ball. See Grace Parks's head position as she swings (photos, page 60).

Keep your left arm straight. The arms must be able to swing freely to create club-head speed. If you strive to keep your left arm straight, it will become rigid and your wrists won't be able to hinge naturally, nor will you create any leverage. As all good players do, keep your arms relaxed and extended in front of your body.

Don't keep your head fixed over the ball! This will lead to a reverse pivot.

WORK ON YOUR SHORT GAME

"Practice your short game!" This is advice you'll hear a lot, and it's worth following. What is your short game? It consists of shots from about one hundred yards out to the green (less if you're not as strong a player), where you are taking less than full swings and trying to get the ball onto the putting surface. Accuracy is at a premium, and you can save a lot of strokes if your short game is sharp.

The clubs you use most often, though not exclusively, around the green are your pitching wedge and sand wedge and your 7-, 8-, and 9-irons. And of course the putter (putting is a huge part of the short game, and you'll take about a third of your strokes on the green).

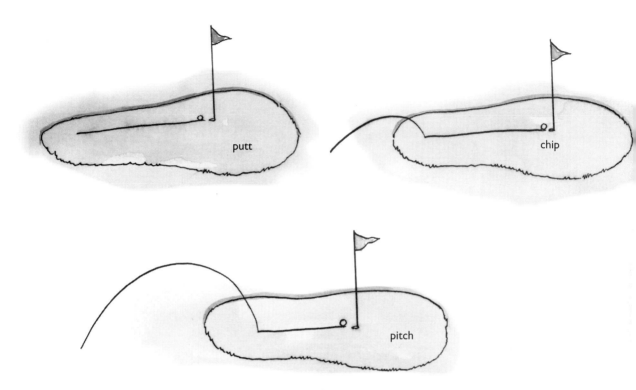

The three most common short game shots.

Putt like a pro

Even if you've never played golf, you've probably played miniature golf. You take a small stroke, using mostly your arms and shoulders, and roll the ball to the hole.

Many new golfers take three and four putts (or more), which quickly destroys a good score. Your goal is to take two putts (or fewer) on every green, which is very attainable for new golfers—much more so than hitting 200-yard drives.

For the most part, putting is a game of preferences. The way you hold the club, the style of the club, and your stance are highly individual. But there are a few basics you should follow.

Although putting grips vary, your palms should face each other, and your thumbs should sit on top of the

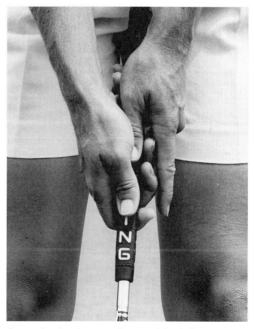

For putting, thumbs go on the top of the shaft, pointing down.

BEST ALL-AROUND PUTTING DRILL

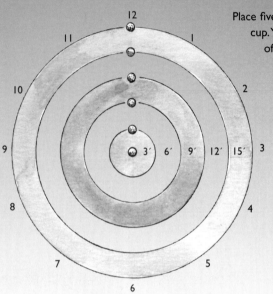

Place five balls in a line at 3-foot intervals 3 to 15 feet from the cup. You start at the 12:00 position, and you must make three of the five putts in order to advance to the 1:00 position. If you make all five putts in a row, you get to skip an hour. Putt the five balls from each position around the clock, 12:00 through 11:00. This drill works on all distances from 3 to 15 feet and from every angle of the hole. It's a great drill to work on all types of putts, and it puts some pressure on your putting, helping you get used to making key putts during a round. To shorten the drill, putt five balls from the 12:00, 3:00, 6:00, and 9:00 positions.

shaft. A popular grip now is called the *cross-handed grip*, where your left hand is below your right on the handle. This style helps keeps unnecessary wrist action out of the stroke.

As in the full swing, set up to the ball so your arms hang naturally. Your eyes should be over the ball.

Make a stroke of equal distance back and through (count one back, two through), similar to a pendulum. Swing your arms from the shoulders and keep your wrists firm (no flipping or buckling). The distance the ball goes is controlled by the length of the backswing. Maintain a smooth and even tempo on all putts.

Keep your head and lower body stock still over the ball until you finish your stroke. This keeps the

Set up with your eyes over the ball.

Above: Keep your wrists firm throughout your putting stroke. **Right:** Aim the putter face squarely at your target.

putter head low to the ground and on the intended path.

The aiming principles are the same as those for the full swing. Aim the club-face squarely at your target, and set your shoulders, hips, and feet parallel to the target line. Swing the putter along the target line.

Chipping and pitching

Chipping, pitching, bunker, flop shots, wedges, and bump and runs. You'll hear many terms for shots taken from close to the green. Don't clutter your mind with this lingo just yet. For now, think in terms of high shots and low shots. *Chips* are low shots that roll more than they fly, or *carry* in golf speak, and *pitches* are higher shots that fly more than they roll.

The chip is a low running shot taken close to the green.

Chipping: master the low shot

A chip is a low shot that lands on the first few feet of the green and rolls to the pin (see drawing page 73). Call it a putt with a flying start. You typically chip from 5 to 20 yards out when you have an unobstructed path to the green.

To get the ball running low and rolling like a putt as soon as possible, your technique needn't vary much from putting. And some players prefer to retain the same grip, stance, and stroke that they use with their putters but simply use a more lofted club such as a pitching wedge or 7-iron, depending on how far they must carry or roll the ball. As a rule, the more roll you need, the less lofted a club you use.

To execute a chip shot, stand very close to the ball, with the club more upright (like a putter), and play the ball toward the back of your stance. Hands start ahead of the ball, your feet and are close together, and your left foot is open to the target (left foot flared to the left). This places your weight more on your left side, which is essential for the shot.

1. Chipping setup position. 2–3. Keep your arms low and extended when chipping.

PITCHING AND CHIPPING DRILL

If you can toss a ball underhand, you can chip and pitch with the best of them. To get a feel for both the chip (low) shot and the pitch (high) shot, try this drill: Have someone hold a club out horizontally to form a bar, and toss the ball toward it. With the low shot, you're throwing the ball under the bar. Notice how your arm stays low and extends in the backswing and follow-through, as it does in a chip shot. With a club in your hands hit the ball under the bar and your arms will naturally do the same thing. Toss the ball over the bar, however, and the arm swing is higher, just as it would be for a pitch shot. Notice how the arm folds on the backswing and follow-through? Try it with a club and you'll get similar results. When you're chipping or pitching, just imagine you're tossing a ball underhand. Picture where you want the ball to land and what the trajectory of the shot will be and trust your swing.

Low = Chip

High = Pitch

Tossing a ball underhand under the bar (top) mimics the motions you'd use on a chip shot, and tossing it underhand over the bar (bottom) mimics the motion of a pitch shot.

CLUB CARRY (AIR TIME) TO ROLL (GROUND TIME) RATIO

pitching wedge	1 to 1
9-iron	1 to 2
8-iron	1 to 3
7-iron	1 to 4
and so on	

Like a putt, the chip shot is an arms and shoulders stroke with a smooth, even tempo—that is, the back and forward swings are made at the same pace—and there's little to no lower body movement. Grip down an inch or two on the handle and focus on contacting the ball first and scuffing the ground second. Keep your wrists quiet throughout the swing. Finish with the club below the hands to keep the ball low.

Don't limit yourself to one club when chipping. All your irons and even a 3-wood can be used. The key is knowing how far the ball will roll with each club. For example, with your pitching wedge the ball will roll about as far as it flies, and with your 7-iron it will roll four times as far. In general, the longer the shot you face, the longer, less lofted a club you use.

The little chart above will help you get a feel for how far the different clubs carry and roll, but you must practice to determine what works best for you.

The pitch: make it a high priority

A pitch is like a mini golf swing, and the ball goes higher than a chip. Call on it when you have to hit over thick grass, knolls, a bunker, or

Above: The pitch is a high, soft approach shot to the green. **Right:** In pitching, the length of swing controls the length of the shot. The photo far right shows a nice follow-through, equal in length to the backswing.

other obstacles to get to the green. For most women it's the shot used 20 to 60 yards from the green. And note that the more you practice your pitching, the better your full swing will be.

There's a subtle weight shift, a little more lower body action, a fuller arm swing, and more wrist hinge than in a chip shot (see photos opposite). Basically your setup is like that of a full swing, except that your stance is a little narrower and maybe slightly open and the ball position is in the middle of your stance. Also be sure the club handle is pointed at your belly button in your setup.

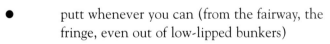

Putt, pitch, or chip?

Some situations can be played with either a high or a low shot. Pick the one you're most confident with. There's more margin for error (a mishit won't stray as far off line) if you get the ball rolling, so you may want to follow this advice when you're near the green:

- putt whenever you can (from the fairway, the fringe, even out of low-lipped bunkers)

- if you can't putt, chip

- if you can't chip, pitch

Sand shots

If you think of the bunker as a sand trap, as it's often referred to, then you'll feel that you can't get out of one. The sand shot intimidates a lot of golfers, but it's really a simple shot. It's unique in that there's actually a thin cushion of sand between the clubface and the ball so that the club never comes in direct contact with the ball.

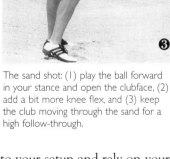

The sand shot: (1) play the ball forward in your stance and open the clubface, (2) add a bit more knee flex, and (3) keep the club moving through the sand for a high follow-through.

Don't overcomplicate this shot. Just make a few adjustments to your setup and rely on your everyday swing. Play the ball forward in your stance with your hands pointed at your belt buckle. Open the clubface first (see photo page 80), then take your grip. Add a bit more knee flex than

To open the clubface, turn the toe of the club out slightly to the right. Think of that clockface. The toe of the bottom edge should be at about 1:00 or 2:00. Always open the clubface first, then take your grip on the club.

usual and lower your hands. Keep the club moving through the sand to a high follow-through. Use your sand wedge, which has a flanged sole to glide through the sand.

Your goal is to enter the sand about an inch or two behind the ball and propel the sand forward onto the green. The ball will come out nicely if you do this. You'll be able to hear the sound of a good sand shot: *thump*. Without a ball, practice splashing the sand high and far out of the bunker and onto the green, taking full swings.

BUILD YOUR CONFIDENCE AROUND FOUR CLUBS

You're allowed to carry fourteen clubs in your bag, but you'll have a more successful start if you build your game and your confidence around the following four. What's more, as a new player, you probably won't see a heck of a lot of difference in the distances your clubs go. As you develop more confidence, skill, and clubhead speed, you will notice a difference and can add more clubs. Right now, though, solid contact and getting the ball in the air consistently are priorities.

Putter. This club is an essential, and you can use it off the green, too, from tightly mown fairway or fringe (I advise you to do so whenever you can!). Practice a lot of 4- to 6-foot putts, which are the ones you'll face a lot. Work on getting the ball within a few feet of the cup on longer putts. Keep your stroke smooth and wrist free.

Pitching wedge. The "PW," as this handy club is also known, is a versatile club. It has a lot of loft, so it's easy to get the ball up in the air (a challenge for many new players). In addition to the high and low shots around the green, you can use it for full swings from the fairway, to get out of tall grass, even from the bunkers for the time being. (Remember, you can master a chip shot with a pitching wedge by keeping your swing short and low. See pages 76–78 on the chip shot.)

6- and 7-irons. Use these midirons versus a harder-to-hit 4- or 5-iron to advance the ball down the fairway. Either is also great off the tee or even to chip with around the green. Learn to hit the ball about 90 to 100 yards and you can advance it well toward the hole. For example, on a 300-yard par 4, divide the hole into manageable chunks of three 100-yard shots, including a tee shot. You'll end up near the green in three shots without using a driver.

5-wood. Use this club off the tee. It's easier to hit than a driver or 3-wood, and you can hit it off the fairway and out of the light rough, as well. You can even chip with this club around the greens for a shot that pops off the clubface and rolls beautifully toward the pin. You can even use it to hit a low shot out from under tree branches. Simply grip down on the club handle and chip out.

PRACTICE MADE PERFECT

Golf swings require upkeep, but most golfers don't spend nearly enough time on the range reinforcing the good setup fundamentals needed to build a repeatable golf swing. You'll enjoy the game more, and so will your playing partners, if you first spend the time at the range to work on making consistent contact. If you don't have time to practice, lower your expectations. And if the only time you "practice" is when you play a round of golf, don't expect quick progress.

A driving range is the perfect place to work on the fundamentals of your swing.

When you do put in the practice time, remember it's quality that counts, not quantity. Try to find thirty minutes a few times a week to work on reinforcing the fundamentals of grip, posture, ball position, and alignment. Mix in drills (see below for suggestions) and games, and don't neglect your short game. Also keep these pointers in mind:

- Don't try to correct too many problems at once. Focus on one or two drills or thoughts, as suggested by your instructor.

- Set up a practice area. Place golf clubs on the ground (one on the target line and one along your toe line) as alignment aids.

- Always have a target.

- Start with shorter clubs and work your way up to your woods.

- Practice the way you play. That is, add some competitive pressure. For example, in short game practice, pick nine different shots from around the green and try to hole the ball in as few shots as possible. Keep score!

Working on your skills need not be limited to a golf course practice range. Your backyard or living room can do very nicely to reinforce fundamentals and develop short game skills. One of my favorite backyard full-swing drills is clipping tees out of the ground. Simply put a tee in the ground about halfway and try to knock it into the air. This will help you work on solid contact.

Indoors is a great place to work on your putting and setup. Swing in front of a mirror to associate what you're seeing with what you're feeling. For putting, lay two clubs on the ground parallel to each other and about three inches apart. Without a ball, practice taking your putter

Feel the coil.

back and through on a straight path.

Here are some more of Krista's other favorite backyard drills.

Feel the coil

Get into your golf posture and hold a volleyball or soccer ball between your hands with your arms extended. Swing your arms back as though you're throwing the ball over your right shoulder. This allows you to feel the rotation of your body as it coils. The motion is very rotary, and the arms swing back up and around. This also builds strength in your upper body, which is important in supporting the club during the swing.

Work on your arm swing

Developing the correct arm swing is one of the most important factors in producing consistency because your arms and the club are the only things that swing. Take your grip with your hands without a club, basically holding on to your left thumb, and swing your arms back so that your thumbs are pointing upward in the backswing (see photos, opposite). Then swing your arms forward, allowing the right arm to rotate over the left, and point your thumbs skyward in the follow-through. You should be able to feel the relaxed and weightless feeling of your arms swinging. Your elbows point down the entire time.

Get a grip

While watching television or talking on the phone, you can practice placing your hands on the club correctly. Grip the club first with the left hand, then place the right hand, making sure both are on the club correctly. Hinge the club up and down a few times, then let go. Repeat twenty times. The more your hands get used to holding the club, the more they will relax when you play, taking tension out of your swing. It

To groove a correct grip, buy a molded practice grip and put it on one of your clubs. You may even want to play with it while you're just starting out is very important to feel the correct grip so it becomes automatic when you play.

Practice your arm swing.

Swing in balance

This balance drill will create the proper blend of arm swing and body rotation in your golf swing. By swinging with your feet together, you'll also swing the club on the correct path to maximize cen-terface contact with the golf club. So grab a 7-iron, place a ball on a tee, put your feet close together, and swing. You should feel the club get light in both directions; let your arms swing freely. You'll be amazed how far you'll hit the ball.

Hear the whoosh

To generate more speed with the arms and teach the hands to hinge the club correctly, hold the club upside down beneath the clubhead and swing with one hand at a time, hearing the club whoosh at the *bottom* of the arc. After you work one hand at a time, put both together and repeat, hearing a whoosh—that's the sound of power.

Swing a broom

To build strength, speed, and the correct swing path, swing a broom. Krista's first coach, Tim Baldwin, previously the women's golf coach at Stanford University, had me doing this drill by the

• •

"If you are making a change in your swing, pose in front of a mirror in these new swing positions. Check them for correctness. Make sure you have the visual image you're trying to accomplish. This will help you associate a feel with a swing move."

—Jackie Bertram Kaufman, lead instructor, Nicklaus/Flick Golf Schools, and director of instruction, TPC at Heron Bay

• •

"The key to advancing in the game is, surprisingly, knowing when to stop practicing. The best advice I ever got was from Peggy Kirk Bell during one of her Golfari all-women's golf schools. I'd been hitting balls and doing drills for hours. I was getting worse and worse and deeply discouraged. She said, 'You know what drill would be the best for you right now? Lifting a cold one—not a club.' She was right."

—Pippin Ross, age 45, writer, handicap 18

time I was 12. It was a favorite of his that he had all his students and players do—a simple drill with tremendous results!

Target a towel

Practice your short game by hitting shots to a towel. Place towels at various known distances and try to land the ball on or close to them.

Chapter 6

YOUR FIRST TIME

In previous chapters we've gone over the parts of the golf course, how to score, and how to swing a golf club. Yeah! You're ready for your first round. Nervous? If you were in Sweden you'd have to pass a playing ability test (one skill is to hit two out of five balls off a tee 80 yards or more) and a written exam on rules and etiquette before being allowed to play on a public course. In the United States, however, if you can pay, you can play.

> "**B**efore you go out on the course without a pro, you should be able to move the ball along with ease and be able to deal with the pace of play."
>
> —Dede Braun, director of instruction, Crystal Springs Golf Course, Burlingame, California

To make the transition from range to course easier, teaching pro Dede Braun tells her students this: "Before you go out on the course without a pro, you should be able to move the ball along with ease and be able to deal with the pace of play." Also, when you're first starting out, take advantage of this unofficial but universally accepted beginner's rule: *Pick up your ball!* If you've hit the ball several more times than your partners and have fallen behind, simply pick up your ball and move it to where the others are hitting from or close to the green, playing in from there. (See sidebar on page 93 for other beginners' rules.)

The **dress code** for golf is fairly conservative: khakis and a polo shirt will do just fine.

PRE-ROUND ROUTINE

Before you can step up to the first tee there are some details you must attend to, from booking a tee time to unloading your golf bag. Ready to roll? Let's go.

Make a tee time

A tee time is simply a reservation to play golf. Just as you'd call to make a dinner reservation at a busy restaurant, you call the golf course pro shop to book a time. You'll be asked what time of day you'd like to play and how many players there will be, from one to four. (Golf is played in groups of four, or foursomes, but you can also request a tee time for three, two, or one player. See pages 123–24 on playing as a single.) You'll be given a precise starting time: 9:48 or 11:09, for example. Courses typically send golfers off in groups of four every eight minutes. Some courses allow ten to fifteen minutes between times—a plus for new golfers who don't want to feel hurried. As a new golfer, request a midweek or late afternoon tee time to avoid the morning rush.

For the best times, call as far ahead as the course allows. Some take reservations thirty days in advance, others a week or a few days. If you're lucky, you can get a tee time for the same day, but don't count on that on busy courses or on weekends. If you're unsure of the dress code, ask when you call. No denim, tank tops, gym shorts, or T-shirts is almost universal policy; see page 43 for more on what to wear.

If you show up at a course without a tee time, you're considered a *walk-on* and will be put on a waiting list or given a tee time, depending on how busy the course is. Walking on is often a good strategy for one or two golfers wanting to get on a popular course.

Try to arrive at the course 30 to 45 minutes before your designated tee time. This will reduce the pressure, giving you ample time to unload your golf bag, change into your golf shoes, pay, warm up, and stock up on snacks.

Drop off your bag

At most courses you'll see a sign near the clubhouse or pro shop that reads "Bag Drop." Drive to this area and unload your golf bag or bags, then park.

Many courses have attendants at the bag drop—it's just like when you pull up outside a hotel lobby and a bellhop takes your bags. He or she will ask your name, what time you're playing, and if you're walking or taking a golf cart. If you're walking, he'll put the bag on a rack where you pick it up after you check in with the pro shop. If you're riding, he'll load it on a golf cart for you.

It's not prohibited to carry your own bag from the parking lot to the drop area, but at high-end places and private clubs it's good form to use the service provided. Tip the person a dollar or two per bag. I like to have plenty of dollar bills in my pocket for tipping.

And don't ever carry your bag into the pro shop or clubhouse. Since your bag will be unattended for a few minutes, take your wallet and other valuables with you.

When should I change into my golf shoes?

Believe it or not, this can be a delicate test of golf etiquette. At a municipal facility or a course with a relaxed atmosphere, some people will put on their golf shoes in the parking lot, but if you're at an exclusive course or a guest at a private club, however, look for a locker room or rest room where you can change into your golf shoes, slather on sunblock, and get ready to

When you arrive at the course, leave your bag at the **bag-drop area** while you park and check in at the pro shop.

play. Since golf shoes have soft plastic spikes rather than metal ones, you can drive in them—I arrive at the course dressed to play from head to toe. That way I don't have to deal with what to do with my street shoes or clothes, since lockers aren't always available.

Check in at the pro shop

Once your bag is in the bag-drop area, head for the pro shop to check in for your tee time and pay your *green fee*—the price of one round of eighteen holes played in one day (some courses offer nine-hole rates). At some courses, the "pro shop" consists of a counter in the clubhouse. Make sure you know whether the green fee includes use of a cart (see also pages 94–96).

Green fees can range from $10 at local municipal courses to $250 or more at a public course or resort facility (these are also called *daily-fee courses*), but there are plenty of courses in the $30 to $75 range. Save your receipt; you might have to show it to an attendant—also known as the *starter*—at the first tee, or hole number 1.

In the pro shop you can also buy balls, gloves, and whatever else you may need for the round.

Ride or walk?

Courses that require golfers to ride in a cart will often include the cart fee in the green fee. I prefer to find a course that allows me to ride or walk as I wish. You can save the cart fee, up to $25 or $40, by walking (beware of courses that don't give you a price break for hoofing it). If you walk, consider renting a pull cart for a few dollars—a two- or three-wheeled trolley for your clubs that you literally pull behind you. That way you don't have to sling your bag over your shoulders.

Another option—most typically available at private clubs and resorts—is a caddie. A caddie is a person hired to carry your bag for the round, but they can also give you valuable advice on yardages, how greens break, and other pertinent information about the course. You pay the pro shop for the service, and you're expected to give a caddie a tip as well, about 35 to 50 percent of the caddie fee.

Using a **pull cart** relieves you of having to carry your bag over your shoulder when walking the course.

There's one more decision to make in the pro shop. If you have time before your tee time, you can "buy" (rent) a bucket of *range balls* for warming up. Most courses have a practice area, or *range*, where you can hit balls (hence *range balls*). The balls typically have black stripes to distinguish them from the balls you play with. Hint: never hit your own balls on the driving range (you don't get them back). And on the practice putting area, use two or three of your own balls rather than the range balls. Some places include range balls in the green fee, but usually you have to pay extra for them.

• •

"**A**s a beginner, I always hoped that the forward tees were up far enough so that the group behind us couldn't see my first drive. I was petrified that I'd whiff a shot or shank one. When I finally did whiff a shot there was, of course, a group of men behind me watching, but I quickly teed up another ball and hit a good drive. After, as I walked down the fairway I realized that the worst had happened and it wasn't so bad."

—Terri Leonard, four-year player, handicap 20

• •

Head to the first tee about five minutes before your tee time.

Countdown to tee time

Once you've taken care of the green fee, head to the practice area if you like. Keep an eye on how much time you have before your tee time.

The *starter* is stationed at the first tee (look for the one with the clipboard and an official air) to get foursomes off in a timely fashion. He or she will tell your group about the course layout, where you can and cannot drive the golf cart, and other information pertinent to your round. Many golf courses have rest rooms only at the clubhouse, so make sure you're prepared by tee time. One member of your group should check in with the starter at least ten minutes before your tee time. Don't report to the first tee until you hear the starter call out your name or the name of a member of your foursome—particularly if the course is busy that day, they're not going to want golfers and

PREGAME CHECKLIST

• • • • • • • • • • • • • • • • • •

Before teeing off, make sure you have these items in your bag or cart.

- golf balls, marked and identified
- tees and ball markers
- glove
- towel
- ball-mark repair tool (see pages 119, 120)
- rain gear
- drinking water
- sunblock, bug repellent, Band-Aids
- hat with a wide brim
- scorecard and pencil
- rule book

To speed play, keep your clubs organized throughout the round. Group woods together, long and midirons in the middle compartment, and short irons up front. The putter can be up front or with the woods.

golf carts clogging the area near the tee. Some courses may have a different procedure for checking in with the starter, so don't be afraid to ask at the pro shop.

Make sure all your equipment is at hand for the round (see sidebar page 89).

TEEING OFF

Drumroll, please. It's the first tee—hole number 1—where you'll hit your first shot of the round. This is a moment of terror for players of all experience levels. Golfers call it first-tee jitters, but it's a classic case of performance anxiety. There are often people watching, so you feel the pressure to make a good impression: no whiffs, no horrible shots. Let's face it: you're in the spotlight, and tension will simply add to a poor performance. A lot of people thrive on this pressure or just don't care if they muff the first shot of the day. I wish I could be that way, but for me it's still the hardest part of the round. Try to focus on what you want to do and not think about what you don't want to do. (See sidebar at right for tips on overcoming first-tee jitters.)

As for first-tee protocol, keep these pointers in mind:

Who goes first? If you want to play by the Rules of Golf, you should flip a coin to determine who has the *honors*—golf talk for who goes first. Most people are less formal and an order is reached by consensus—usually whoever's ready. It will speed play if those in your foursome playing the back tees go first and those playing the forward tees—all beginners!—go last.

Stand outside the peripheral vision of the person hitting and don't talk or move while someone else is swinging the club; wait until after they hit to walk or drive forward to your tee.

Identify your ball. You should know the brand name and number of the ball you're playing with (Titleist 1, Pinnacle 3, for example) and what balls your playing partners are using. There's a good reason for this. If you mistakenly hit someone else's ball at any time during the round, it can be a two-stroke penalty. If two or more of you are playing with the same kind of ball, initial your ball with a pen or pencil.

Spot balls. You should always pay attention to where someone's tee shot goes so you

Top: Make sure you know what brand and model ball you're hitting so you don't hit another player's by mistake. **Center:** Tee up the ball no more than two club lengths behind the markers and never in front of them. **Above:** Those little wooden pegs with the concave top? Those are tees. Stick one of them in the ground and put your ball on top of it. The tee box is the only place you're allowed to use a tee. Tee the ball high with drivers, medium with fairway woods, and low with irons.

CONQUERING FIRST-TEE JITTERS

Here are some tips to minimize the fear and intimidation of the first tee.

A golfer's pocket equipment: glove, tees, an extra ball, a ball-mark repair tool, and a ball marker or coin.

- Be prepared. If you're fumbling for stuff in your bag, you'll add to the tension level. Take everything you'll need for the round out of your golf bag and put it in the cart's front compartment. I put several balls, extra tees, my sunblock, water, and a snack there. Whether I'm riding or walking, I always have my "pocket equipment": an extra ball in case I hit one out-of-bounds, a few tees, my ball marker for the greens (I use a dime). You want to play efficiently and not run back and forth between your ball and your bag. This is a good practice throughout the round.

- There may be times when you'll be paired with total strangers. Accept this. It's part of golf and can make it fun. I know many women, including me, who dread this. Don't apologize for your game, but simply say that you're a new golfer and this is your first time out.

- If you're a new golfer, play from the most forward set of tees from hole 1, which gives you the shortest distance to the hole (see chapter 4). Continue playing from the same color tee boxes throughout the round.

- Relax. To play your best golf, you need to be as loose as a noodle, so as you step up to hit the ball, take a deep breath. Focus on what you want to do (hit the ball onto the fairway), not on what you don't want to do (whiff the ball or hit it into the water).

- Use your favorite club for a confidence boost—an iron or a high-lofted wood—whatever you're comfortable with. Have the club handy so you're ready to step up to the tee when it's your turn.

- If despite your best efforts you wind up muffing your first shot, ask the other members of your foursome if you can "take a *mulligan*"—a time-honored first-tee tradition. A mulligan is essentially a free second shot if you mis-hit your first one. Most courses frown on mulligans because they slow down play, and of course they're against the rules, but they can be just what you need to get off the tee with confidence.

can help locate it or advise them to play a provisional ball if the first one looks as if it went out-of-bounds or deep into trees (see chapter 8 on rules). Carry this courtesy throughout the round on all shots. Balls are easily lost in leaves and tall grass.

Tee up the ball between the markers and no more than two club lengths behind them. It's against the rules to tee it up in front of them. Look for a level spot and follow the adage, "tee up with trouble." That is, if there are bunkers, water, woods, or other hazards running along the right side of the fairway, tee up your ball on the right side of the tee box and aim away from these areas.

SPEEDING UP PLAY

On some golf courses, signs help you monitor your pace of play.

Whether you're a fast player or not, as a woman you'll likely be stereotyped as slow. So don't be surprised if course rangers ask you to pick up the pace or skip a hole just because you're a woman.

Here are some tips to help you keep up. An eighteen-hole round of golf should take four hours or less, though I've known rounds to go five hours. Some courses have a clock that says you should be at a particular hole in a specified amount of time. A good rule of thumb is twelve to fifteen minutes per hole in a foursome.

- Keep the group ahead of you within sight, and wait until the players are just out of your range before you hit.
- Play when you're ready even if you're not away and don't have the honors. Just make sure nobody is in the line of fire (see page 93).
- Take only *one* practice swing—there's nothing more irritating to other players than someone who takes more than a few practice swings.
- Carry an extra ball in your pocket so you don't have to go back to the cart if you hit a ball out-of-bounds or lose it in a water hazard.
- Take more than one club to your ball from the cart. If you're hitting a shot onto the green, take your putter so you can proceed directly to the green.
- Take the cart and/or pull carts near the back side of the green, nearest to the next tee, so you can exit the green quickly after you *putt out* (all players have holed their putts).
- Mark your scorecard at the next tee, not on the putting green. As soon as you putt out, clear off the green from the back or side as quickly as possible to allow the next group to hit into the green.
- Spot the ball for your playing partners and yourself. Follow it into rough or out-of-bounds. If you think your ball can't be found, hit a provisional ball (see page 113). If your partner loses a ball, hit yours first, then help look for it.
- Limit a lost ball search to two minutes, even though the rules allow five: this isn't the U.S. Open. If you're determined to find your ball, let a faster group *play through* (basically, leapfrog your group).
- Assess your shot and choose your club while others are hitting.
- Be prepared to let the next group play through at the next convenient spot (the tee or fairway) if they're able to play faster.

WHO GOES FIRST?

After the first hole, the person with the lowest score on the previous hole has the honors on the tee. If it's a tie, the person with the honors from the previous hole carries on. In the fairway or on the green (essentially anywhere else on the course but the tee box) the rules stipulate that the golfer who is farthest from the hole—called being *away*—should play first. In competition, *always* follow these rules for the order of play.

A big "however," however. In the interest of faster play, many golfers agree to play *ready golf*, and in informal rounds I heartily recommend it. Basically this means you don't stand on ceremony. The golfer who's ready goes first, even if he or she is not away and doesn't have the tee honors. Always make sure there's no one directly in front of you. It's good to play fast, but you must play safely, too.

PUTTING

On and around the putting green is another area that makes new golfers nervous. What do I do? How do I act? What do I do with the flagstick (the pin)? As you play more you'll pick up the nuances, but here's a quick lesson.

The golfer whose ball is farthest from the hole putts first. (Ready golf typically isn't as necessary on the greens.) If all balls are on the putting surface, the player whose ball is closest to the hole either pulls or tends the pin and putts last. Per USGA rules, if a player is just off the green on the fringe (see page 48) and ten

Take turns **tending the flagstick**. Stand at arm's length from the pin on the same side as any shadow and hold the flag down so it doesn't flap. As the ball moves toward the hole, pull the pin out. Alternatively, you may remove the pin and lay it off to the side before anyone putts.

(see page 48)

BEGINNERS' RULES

Perhaps it's better to say *beginners rule*: when you're a new golfer (or a high handicapper), you can get away with murder on the golf course as long as you're a speedy and courteous player. Bone up on the finer points of etiquette outlined in chapter 8 and forget about the USGA's Rules of Golf for now. Unless you're playing in a formal event or tournament, you can adhere to the following "rules." Your playing partners will thank you.

- Don't keep score.
- Improve your lie— that is, move the ball from deep rough or any other pesky lie.
- Tee up the ball in the fairway—this will help you get the ball airborne.
- Pick up your ball after six or seven shots if you still haven't reached the green; on the green, take no more than three putts.

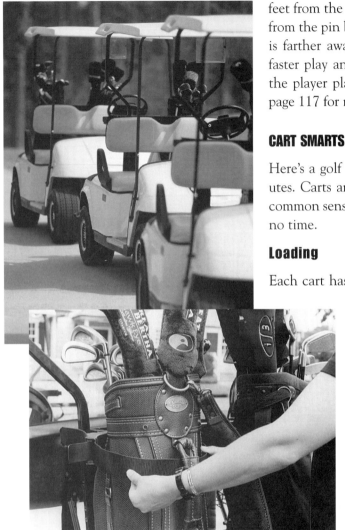

feet from the pin and another player is twenty-five feet from the pin but on the putting surface, the player who is farther away goes first. However, in the interest of faster play and invoking the rules of ready golf, often the player playing from the fringe would go first. See page 117 for more information on putting protocol.

CART SMARTS

Here's a golf skill you can master in about three minutes. Carts are easy to drive, and if you apply a little common sense you'll be zooming around confidently in no time.

Loading

Each cart has room for two people and two golf bags. Designate a driver and strap his or her bag onto the back of the cart on the driver's side. Make sure the cart strap is securely fastened around your bag so it can't fall off the back—an embarrassing rookie moment.

Driving

Carts, like cars, have keys, and you must be sixteen years old to drive one. Either the person taking your green fee will give you the ignition key or it will be in the cart. Turn the key to the "On" position and keep it there for the entire round. As in a car, the accelerator pedal is on the right and the brake pedal is on the left. When you press down on the accelerator, the cart will start moving. Steer it just like a car, and put the brake pedal to the floorboard to stop and secure the cart. To start up again, push the accelerator pedal. To go in reverse, shift the lever under the seat from Forward to Reverse; the cart will make a beeping noise like a truck backing up.

Top: Driving a golf cart is one of the more easily mastered aspects of the game. **Above:** Make sure the cart strap is securely fastened before driving off.

Cart courtesy

- There are three places you never take a cart: onto or within thirty yards of the putting surface; onto the tee box (though I've seen it happen); and through a

LINKS LINGO

- **Links.** Informal term for the golf course. To golf purists, *links* are seaside courses in the British Isles.
- **Fore!** The golfer's universal warning for "look out!" and it's what you yell when you hit an errant shot that could endanger another golfer. If you hear "Fore!," cover your head and stay put until the ball has landed.
- **Mulligan.** A free second shot on the first tee.
- **That's a gimme,** or **that's good.** For putts of less than 2 feet your opponent or partner may say "that's good" or "that's a gimme," meaning she'll give you that shot without your having to actually putt (you can't give yourself a gimme). Always accept it and say "thank you." It's a courteous gesture that also speeds up play.
- **You're away.** You are farthest from the hole and should hit first.
- **You have the honors.** You've earned the right to tee off first by having the low score on the previous hole.
- **Let's play ready golf.** Don't stand on ceremony by playing honors golf. Play when you're ready to go even if your ball is closer to the hole.
- **Front nine.** Holes I through 9.
- **Back nine.** Holes 10 through 18.
- **The turn.** When you've finished the front nine and before you tee off at hole 10, you're at the turn. Some courses have a halfway house, which is the place to make a quick stop to grab a snack and use the rest room. Don't take more than five minutes or you could lose your turn.
- **The 19th hole.** The bar or restaurant, generally in the clubhouse, where you head after your round for a drink or a bite to eat. If you got lucky and had a hole-in-one, you're expected to buy a drink for everyone there.

bunker. Most courses have a concrete or gravel cart path and well-marked signs and roped-off areas indicating where you can and cannot drive. Some courses might put a "90-degree" rule into effect. This means you can drive onto the fairway but only on a perpendicular line from the cart path or rough to your ball (the shortest distance). After you hit, take the same line back to the cart path and proceed to your next shot.

- Don't park too close to another player and her ball. You may interfere with her swing or her vision.

- Don't move the cart while another player is hitting.

- When walking to your ball from the cart, take several clubs with you so you don't have to go back to the cart for another club.

- When approaching the green, drive the cart around to the back of the green where it's closest to the next tee so you can vacate the green quickly for the next group. (The same courtesy holds true if you're pulling a hand cart or carrying your bag.)

- If you're riding with another player, drop her off at her ball and drive to your ball to get ready to hit. (If the distance gap is more than about 50 yards, wait for the other player to hit; otherwise she can catch up with you on foot.)

PEOPLE YOU'LL SEE ALONG THE WAY

During your round you might encounter some of these folks.

The one group of people you are assured of seeing on any golf course is *other golfers*. Keep these simple rules in mind. Keep up with the group in front of you. Try not to look over your shoulder and fret about the group playing behind you. As long as you keep the group in front in eyesight, no worries. If your group falls behind, let faster groups play through.

On some courses, especially busy ones, *rangers* (also called *marshals* or *player assistants*) make the rounds of the course in carts identified by a flag or sign. They're there to make sure play is proceeding apace. They might help you look for lost balls, rake bunkers—anything to keep things moving.

At many courses, a person drives around all day offering sodas, water, beer, crackers, sandwiches, hot dogs, and the like from a beverage cart. You have to pay, and it's polite to give the cart attendant a small tip.

AFTER THE ROUND

Your group has just putted out on the 18th hole. Shake hands around your foursome and say, "I enjoyed playing with you." Now go back to the clubhouse area and return your cart. There may be an attendant there to clean off your clubs with a towel. It's best not to resist. Give him a buck or two for the service, then head to the "19th hole"—the bar or restaurant where food and beverages are served—to reward yourself for a job well done.

Chapter 7

I hope your coach has taught you not only swing fundamentals but also a thing or two about playing golf, because playing your best does not mean just swinging your best. "Women tend to get hung up on being perfectionists with their swings," says golf pro Krista Dunton. "But you can play well if you focus on your target and make smart choices about what shots to hit and what clubs to use." Remember the typing versus writing analogy from LPGA master professional Annette Thompson? Just because you can type (swing a club) doesn't mean you can write (play the game).

A phrase you'll hear bandied about as you learn to play the game is *course management*. In a nutshell, it means playing the most appropriate shot for any given situation according to your skill level. It's not just poor swings but poor decision making that can lead to a high score. Remember, when you're on the golf course, keep your mind on your task, which is to get the ball into the cup in as few strokes as possible. Here are some tips on how to do just that.

WHICH CLUB SHOULD I HIT?

You're bound to fall in love with one club when you're first starting out. A 7-iron is a favorite of many new golfers. For me it was my 5-iron. I used it off the tee and on every shot in the fairway until I got near enough to the green to hit my pitching wedge, my next-favorite club. This is a good confidence-boosting strategy, but you don't want to get stuck in a rut where you're afraid to

• •

"Learn to hit your 5-wood off the tee. A good tee shot builds confidence and sets you up for the remainder of the hole. A 5-wood has more loft than a long iron, so it's easier to hit, plus the club is lighter and the length of the club gives you added distance when hit correctly. When you master the 5-wood off the tee, then try the 3-wood. In the fairway use a 5- or 6-iron that you can hit fairly straight and with some distance. Even if you hit your 5- or 6-iron 100 or 110 yards, in two to three fairway shots you will be near the green and ready for a little pitch shot and a putt or two."

—Krista Dunton, LPGA and PGA teaching professional

• •

use other clubs. To make progress, you must learn to hit both woods and irons well. But if you're just starting out, use this simple formula: use a 3- or 5-wood off the tee, a 6- or 7-iron in the fairway, and a pitching or sand wedge around the greens. That's enough clubs to get you going. As your game improves and you add more to your bag, you'll need to figure out what to hit when.

How far do my clubs go?

At first you'll likely hit all your clubs about the same distance, but as you start making solid, *centerface contact*, you'll notice a difference in the distance you hit each one. For example, I used to hit my 7-iron 90 yards. Now it's my 105-yard club, which is a lot less distance than my rookie sister hits her 7-iron. But don't get hung up on how far you're supposed to hit a club or compare yourself with other players.

Each club is designed to go a different distance (there are typically 5- to 10-yard gaps between successive irons and woods). You should know how far, on average, you hit each club. To do so, determine what club you hit 100 yards, and calculate distances for your other clubs based on that figure. For example, say you hit your 7-iron 100 yards. You can then assume you'll hit your 8-iron 90 yards and your 6-iron 110 yards. Make a little cheat sheet to tuck into your golf bag. Golfers with slower swing speeds will notice less difference in distance between their longer clubs.

What does taking "more" or "less" club mean?

The most common error among amateurs is that they don't *take enough club* to get them where they want to go. It's always better to take "more" club than you think you need and swing smoothly than to take "less" club and swing out of your shoes. "More club" simply means you choose a club that's designed to go farther, which means a club with a lower number. For example, a 5-iron is more club than a 6-iron. Taking less club is just the opposite. When you opt for a

9-iron over a 7-iron you're taking less club. In short, as the numbers on the clubs get higher, the distances the clubs are designed to go gets shorter.

Calculating distance

In deciding which club to hit, the first step is figuring out how far you are from your target, which could be the green or an area of the fairway. Pick a club that you know you hit that distance (see above). Golf courses give you clues on how far you are from the flagstick so you can figure out what club to use. However, there are other factors to consider—wind conditions, for example—before picking the club to hit.

Some courses have precise **yardage markers** scattered around the fairway, indicating the distance to the middle of the green.

Look at the scorecard. It gives you the total distance from tee to green (see page 53). This information is useful on par-3 holes, where you have a chance to get the ball to the green with your tee shot. (You can also use the figure to calculate how long your tee shot was on a monster drive on par 4s and 5s.)

Find the yardage markers. There are three standard yardage markers on golf courses, which indicate the distance to the middle of the green. From 200 yards out there will be a blue disk in the middle of the fairway; from 150 yards it's white; and from 100 yards, red. This is an almost universal color code. Also note that the 150-yard marker is often a white post in the middle of the fairway, which usually makes a very nice target off the tee. You'll also often find additional yardages indicated on markers scattered around the fairway (see photo above).

Check the pin location. Many players are surprised to learn that the pin, or flagstick, location is changed frequently in order to help keep the green evenly worn. If the pin is toward the back of the green it may add 10 or more yards to your shot, affecting your choice of club. To indicate where the pin's relative location is, courses might use red, white, and blue flags. If the flag on the pin is red, the pin is close to the front of the green; a white flag indicates a middle pin

TAKE A HIKE!

Who says golf isn't exercise? An average golf course is more than 6,000 yards long, which is about 3½ miles. So if you have the option to walk the course, do! Your thighs and your heart will thank you.

If your ball is in deep rough, take a club with a lot of loft and play the ball back in your stance.

location; and blue, toward the back. Or they may give you a photocopied *pin sheet* on the first tee, which will tell you the yardage from the front of the green to the pin. Pay attention! Since greens can be 30 yards deep or more, the flagstick's location relative to the green depth will affect your club selection and could mean the difference between a birdie and a bogey.

Assess the conditions. Yardage alone doesn't always determine distance. You have to factor in the conditions as well. Is it windy? A brisk wind in your face can in effect add 20 yards or more to a shot. An uphill target usually calls for more club as well. Your lie (the way the ball is sitting in the grass) can affect the distance the ball travels. So, for example, the yardage marker in the fairway may say you are 110 yards from the green. But the green is uphill (add 10 yards) and the wind is in your face (add 10 more yards), so you have to play the club that you hit 130 yards, not 110.

STROKE SAVERS

Now that you know how to choose your weapons, it's time to learn how to turn triple bogeys into pars. Here are some ideas that have been useful to me as I've developed as a golfer. I hope they'll help you too.

Get loose

One sure way to lower your scores is to warm up and stretch before you play. If you step onto the tee cold, your muscles will be tight, restricting your range of motion. You could injure yourself, and your score on the first few holes will suffer (see Pre-Round Stretching Exercises, pages 102–5). This doesn't mean you have to get to the golf course an hour before your round to hit balls. Who has time? Just do some warm-up stretches and light aerobics to get your blood flowing—LPGA Hall of Famer Nancy Lopez walks on the treadmill for a half hour to get her juices going.

Develop a preshot routine

Think of the Women's National Basketball Association star Sheryl Swoopes before a free throw or tennis ace Martina Hingis before a serve: each has a little routine that helps her get in the moment and focus. It's the same in golf. All the pros go through a *preshot routine* to get them into the ready mode to swing the club. Routines vary, but they all have the same basic elements: assessing your lie, picking a target, taking a practice swing, aiming the clubface at the target, and aligning your body parallel to the target line.

The routine helps you get in the trust mode, says Krista Dunton. She likens it to when you learned to drive—fasten seat belt, check the mirrors, hands at ten and two, remember to signal before the turn. Now you drive from one point to the next, sometimes not even sure how you got there. A preshot routine in golf allows you to relax and stay focused on the target while making sure that the essentials of grip, alignment, ball position, posture, and stance are in place. Practice a routine and keep it quick (30 seconds, tops) and consistent.

Get the ball rolling

Say you're 10, 20, 30 yards from the green: should you putt, chip, or pitch? Choose the shot that requires the smallest amount of "swing" and that gets the ball rolling soonest, which reduces the margin of error. Putting from off the green—as much as 10 yards or more—is my secret weapon, and many teaching pros advise this tactic. I do it whenever I can, but the conditions have to be right. If the grass is too bumpy, your ball will roll off line and it will be very difficult to judge how big a stroke to take. To make the decision easier, remember this maxim: if you can't putt—say there's a knoll to clear—then chip, and if you can't chip—say there's a bunker between your ball and the green—then pitch.

Avoid the big number

Avoid big numbers on your scorecard by getting out of trouble and back into the fairway in one shot. Only attempt a recovery shot you can execute.

This may sound obvious, but the surest way to shoot lower scores is to avoid shooting higher ones. If you're in the rough, a pesky bunker, or some other trouble spot, your goal is to get out of trouble and back into the fairway in one shot. The safest route out is not always the most direct one—you may have to play laterally into the fairway, not forward toward the hole. Always play the percentages by attempting a recovery shot that you know you can hit. One of my favorite tips for less-experienced players is from Katherine Marren, senior instructor at Pebble Beach Golf Academy. She advises people in a situation that calls for a shot beyond their skill level to take an *unplayable lie* (see page 113). You'll incur a one-stroke penalty, but you'll be able to play the ball from a more desirable location.

Keep the ball in play

Imagine where you want to go (fairways and greens), not where you don't want to go (water, sand, and rough). Of course, the best way to stay out of trouble is to aim away from it. This thinking should start on the first tee. What side of the fairway is it best to be on? Where is the trouble? Are there out-of-bounds? Bunkers? Trees?

Try "teeing up with trouble"—that is, if bunkers are on the right of the fairway, tee up on the right side of the tee box and aim away from the trouble spot.

PRE-ROUND STRETCHING EXERCISES

—Alan R. Klein, MSPT

Alan R. Klein is the director of Physical Therapy Services of Huntington, New York, a state-of-the-art clinic specializing in the prevention and treatment of golf-related and other sports injuries.

It's key to warm up and stretch before you play golf to maximize your performance on the course as well as decrease your risk of injury. Below are six simple stretches that you can do before and during your round to get and keep your golf muscles in the swing. But before you perform any stretching exercise, make sure you understand the following guidelines.

- Warm up before you stretch. Walk briskly or take an easy jog (try parking at the far end of the parking lot at the course) so that you increase your body temperature and break a light sweat. However, your warm-up should not be so intense that it causes fatigue.

- Move slowly and carefully into each stretch, maintaining it for 15 to 30 seconds or longer. Avoid bouncing and quick, jerky motions.

- Breathe normally, but when moving deeper into the stretch, focus on your exhalation.

- Repeat the stretch for your opposite side when indicated.

- Never force muscles or joints beyond their normal range of motion. You should never feel any pain while stretching.

- Try to do the stretching exercises before, during, and after you practice or play a round of golf.

- Incorporate your stretching program into your daily activities at work and at home.

Standing Side Stretch

While standing upright using good posture, hold the golf club over your head in both hands, elbows bent slightly. Gently lean to one side until you feel a mild stretch along the opposite side of your body. While leaning over, make sure your hips are straight and even. Repeat for the opposite side, again taking care not to overstretch.

Standing side stretch.

Armless Warm-Up and Stretch

Cross your arms over your chest and position yourself as if addressing a golf ball, maintaining the correct spine angle and posture. Slowly, carefully, and gently stretch into your backswing while maintaining a stable right leg (left if you're left-handed). Keep your eyes on the ball and hold your backswing stretch 15 to 30 seconds or longer. When you've finished stretching into your backswing, slowly start to rotate your body, keeping your arms crossed, till you reach the follow-through position. As you feel yourself begin to warm up, you can slowly increase the speed at which you're doing the exercise while decreasing the time you hold the stretch at the end ranges.

Armless warm-up and stretch.

Standing Hamstring Stretch

Lift one leg and foot onto a stable surface at about knee height, with standing leg straight. (It's extremely important to understand how to stretch your hamstrings—the back of your thigh—correctly. Your hamstrings are connected to your pelvis, and you can injure your back by stretching with incorrect form.) Your back should not be overly arched or bent forward. Tuck your butt under your body, which flattens your lower back and protects it from injury. Keep your foot pointed downward and your knee bent to better isolate your hamstrings, at the same time minimizing the stretch to your calf. Once you're in position, lean forward to your hips, keeping your back straight. As you lean forward you'll feel your hamstrings start to stretch. As you gain flexibility, you can modify this exercise by slowly trying to straighten your knee, keeping your foot pointed downward. If you perform this stretch with your knee straight and start to bring your foot up (toes toward your nose), you'll feel a stretch in the back of your upper and lower leg. Repeat for the opposite leg. The higher the surface your foot is on, the more stretch you'll feel in the back of your leg and hamstrings.

(continued next page)

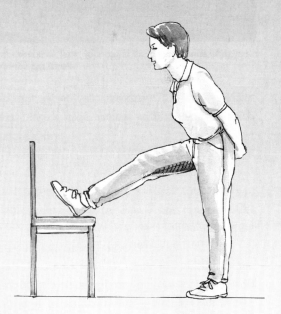

Standing hamstring stretch.

PRE-ROUND STRETCHING EXERCISES

. . . .

(continued from previous page)

Standing Calf Stretch with Knee Straight

Stand at arm's length from a solid support. Make sure you have good posture, keeping your back straight. Put one foot forward and one foot back. The back leg is the one you'll be stretching. Keep the heel of the back foot on the ground with your foot facing as directly forward as you're capable of. Keeping your back straight, bend your elbows and your forward knee while moving your hips forward. As you start to stretch the calf of the back leg, don't let your ankle turn inward or outward. It's important to keep your joints and body in correct alignment while stretching. Start this exercise very slowly. You'll feel a stretch in your calf and possibly the front of your ankle.

Achilles Tendon Stretch with Knee Bent

Stand at arm's length from a solid support. Make sure you have good posture, keeping your back straight. Put one foot forward and one foot back. The back leg is the one you'll be stretching. Keep the back knee slightly bent so you'll be better able to isolate your Achilles tendon (the lower part of the back of your leg). Repeat for the opposite leg.

Standing calf stretch with knee straight.

Achilles tendon stretch.

Wrist Flexion and Extension Stretch

Good flexibility in the wrist and forearm is important for preventing tendonitis and overuse syndromes involving the elbow and wrist. With your elbows straight, grasp the palm of your hand with your opposite hand and gently bend your wrist into extension until you feel stretching in the muscles on the palm side of your forearm. For the opposite stretch (into flexion), keep your elbows straight and bend your wrist by pushing gently with your opposite hand on the top portion of the hand you're stretching.

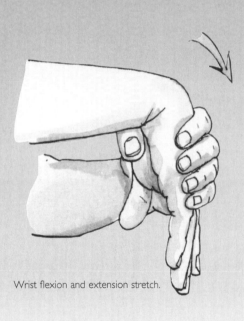
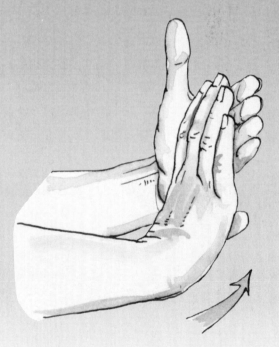

Wrist flexion and extension stretch.

Contact information for Alan Klein is in chapter 10, Resources.

"Long means wrong"

I don't remember where I heard this phrase, but I wish I could properly credit it, because it's one of my favorites. The more time you stand over your ball, the more likely you are to hit a poor shot. In other words, the more you think about *how* you want to hit the ball—a recipe for tension—rather than *where* you want to hit it, the harder it will be to perform. Trust me: it's true. Darlene Sommers, a teaching professional at Hillendale Golf Course in Ithaca, New York, puts it more "delicately": "The more you think, the more you stink!"

Stay with one swing thought

When you're standing over the ball ready to play, ten swing thoughts—keep your knees flexed, your wrists hinged, and so on—spell disaster. It's best to stick to one simple thought when you're on the golf course: "follow through," "complete your backswing," or "don't rush the swing," for example. You can also do a quick preswing alignment or grip check. Are my shoulders parallel to the target line? Is my heel pad on top of the club? Then trust yourself and swing the club with your target in mind.

· ·

"Woods give you more confidence and are great for women. I use my 11-wood instead of a 5-iron because the 11-wood tends to get the ball up in the air a little bit faster and it lands very softly. When you're looking down at a long iron there doesn't look like there's much loft, so you try to make the ball go up in the air instead of just swinging the club. When you're looking down at a club and you see a lot of loft on it—particularly with an 11-wood—it's much easier to swing the club and get the feeling of the club doing the work as opposed to your trying to help get the ball up in the air. Plus in the rough it's great because with an iron your hosel tends to get caught up in the grass and can hook a lot of shots [a shot that goes sharply to the left], whereas if you've got some mass in the clubhead, as you do with a fairway wood, you can hit some pretty good shots out of there.

"To have success hitting woods, always try to maintain good tempo and sweep the grass, just letting the ball get in the way. With irons it's more of a hit down, taking a divot. Women, because of their physical makeup, generally are sweepers of the ball more than hitters."

—Stephanie Brecht, 13-year LPGA Tour professional

· ·

"**W**hat do I find hard about the game? That's easy. The same competitive side of my personality that keeps me hitting the links is the side that cringes every time I duff one in the water or wormburn one down the fairway. I hate how easy it is to feel like Annika Sorenstam one moment and a complete novice the next."

—Amy DiAdamo, 20-something, avid golfer

Develop a "safety valve" swing

This is a tip I learned from former LPGA Tour pro Janet Coles on a photo shoot for *Golf For Women* magazine, and it's one I use all the time. A *safety valve swing*, as Coles calls it, is a shot you know you can hit consistently—call it old faithful. If you're having a bad day on the course, where every shot either skitters along the ground or darts to the right, bring out your safety swing. For mine, I play the ball closer to my right foot (like a chip shot) and take a three-quarter swing, which promotes good contact. Sometimes I hit it so well I wonder why I don't do it all the time.

Divide and conquer

Here's one of the most important lessons a new player can learn: distance is not the enemy; swinging too hard and out of control is. Most golfers, when faced with a daunting distance in front of them, will grab their longest club, grip it really tight, and take a big, fast swing. Typically the

GREEN READING: AS EASY AS ABC

The ball doesn't always roll to the hole on a straight path. The slope of the green influences how fast or slow the ball will roll and how it will *break* (move) right or left.

One of the best ways to get a feel for the slope of the green is to look at its contours from about 5 to 10 feet away as you approach the green. Imagine water flowing over the green: it will always flow from high to low. The same happens with putts. If you keep the ball rolling on the high side, it has a good chance of going in, but once the ball hits the low side of the hole, the ball never has a chance of going in.

Find the high side of the hole, visualize how the ball will roll (imagine you're rolling the ball underhand), and make a smooth putting stroke. If you can see it, you can sink it!

—Krista Dunton

Determine how your ball will *break* (the direction it will roll) before you line up your putt.

HELP! I CAN'T HIT MY FAIRWAY WOODS!

You're not alone. Though you'll often hear that woods are easier to hit than irons, not all golfers would agree. Woods are longer and take some getting used to, but they're lighter and when you hit them correctly the ball will go farther. I like to have new players swing a fairway wood early because it encourages them to swing the club and be aggressive; this way they never develop a preference for irons or woods. Players who struggle with woods typically play the ball too close to the middle of their stance, with their hands ahead of the ball. The ball is played in the forward part of the stance (inside the left heel), and this encourages the club to contact the ball slightly on the upswing.

Irons are shorter, with more weight at the clubhead. Since the shaft is relatively short, you stand closer to the ball, which encourages you to swing the club on a more descending angle. Also, the ball is just slightly forward of center in your stance, encouraging a downward blow.

—Krista Dunton

"The driving range is where you train your golf swing. The golf course is where you go out and trust what you've trained. When you think on the golf course, do so before it's your turn to hit and before you address the ball. For example, in order to speed up play, do all of your preparatory work before it's your turn: where your target is, how far you have, what type of shot you'll have, what club you'll use. . . . Visualize the shot. When you pick a club it will be much easier, having thought of those questions. Once you have a club in hand, it's time to trust and react. If you were tossing a ball of paper into a wastepaper basket, you'd just look and throw. Use this approach with golf: have a picture of what you're trying to do, pick out a target, and react."

—Krista Dunton

ball dribbles about 25 yards in front of them (this is known as a *wormburner*). If you're faced with a long hole, you don't need to hit your longest club off the tee or in the fairway. Choose one that's easier for you to hit. Think about it: you can go the same distance using a 5-wood and 7-iron as you can with a driver and wedge. And if you know you can't possibly reach a green even with your best shots, divide the hole into manageable chunks. A 345-yard par 4 is just three shots of 115 yards. With a one-putt you can still make par.

Laying up (deliberately landing short of the green), is another way to take the fear out of long distances. On par 3s, for example, there is no rule that says you have to get to the green in one shot. If you don't like your odds of reaching a par-3 green with your tee shot, play the ball to a safe landing area short of the green. You should also consider laying up short of trouble on par 4s and 5s if you're not confident you can clear it.

UNLEASHING THE BIRDIE GOLFER IN YOU

It's every golfer's dream to shoot a perfect round: eighteen birdies for a score of 54. It's never been done, but Pia Nilsson, the longtime head coach of the Swedish national golf team and cofounder with Lynn Marriott of Coaching for the Future golf schools at the Legacy Resort (Phoenix, Arizona), believes it's possible. Below is a list she developed for some of the world's elite players to help them achieve that goal. It's great advice for any golfer hoping to play to her potential. Learn to

1. play with all your clubs
2. play a straight shot, slice, hook, draw, fade, high shot, low shot, punch shot
3. play different types of chips, pitches, and bunker shots suitable for different lies, greens, and flag positions
4. read greens and putts on all different types of grass
5. choose the best shot around the green on different types of grass
6. play whether it's hot, cold, wet, or windy
7. play whether the pace of play is fast or slow
8. play on different types of courses
9. use the right strategy for the course on which you are playing
10. play with people who are pleasant and people who you don't think you have much in common with
11. play from divots; uphill, downhill, and sidehill lies; sand; rough; and pine needles
12. play with or without spectators
13. be just as sharp in the first round as the last and on the first hole as well as the last
14. see, hear, and feel that the ball is going to the hole
15. be 100 percent focused on the target when you hit the ball
16. be motivated regardless of the importance of the tournament
17. be aware of your emotions and manage them well
18. trust yourself, your swing, and the shot you have chosen to hit

Think tempo, not technique

Put a driver in a golfer's hands and most will take a fast, out-of-control swing in an effort to crush it. Ditto for woods and long irons. Although women need to work on swinging with more acceleration, it's key to maintain a smooth tempo while doing so. Think of it this way: you should swing your driver and pitching wedge at the same level of effort.

Here's a great drill that Krista Dunton has her students do to improve the tempo and rhythm of their swings. This applies to all shots, from putts to chips, pitches, and full swings. She calls it the 1-2-3-4 drill.

"I love the feeling of hitting a good shot (especially a drive) and the confidence I feel when I'm playing well. When my game is off, however, I hate the way I become a bit of a sulk. I lose my confidence and start to worry I'll never get my game back on track. The more I worry, the worse it gets. I tell myself I should be enjoying the game no matter what. This is one area I really need to work on."

—Terri Leonard, four-year player, handicap 20

Once you have set up to the ball, look at your target and count *1*; then look back to the ball and count *2*; the backswing is *3*; and the follow-through swing is *4*. Keep the pace of the counting the same for 1 through 4—I guarantee this will help the flow of your swing and keep your mind free of mechanical thoughts, ensuring better results.

Play your game

You must manage your game according to your skill level. Play to your strengths (using an iron off the tee, for example). This may sound obvious, but you'd be surprised how many golfers attempt a shot because they think it's the one they *should* hit (e.g., "I'm on the tee so I must use my driver"). If this strategy means playing all shots with your 7-iron, so be it. And set reasonable goals for yourself. If you're not capable of reaching a par 4 in two with your two best shots, don't put pressure on yourself to do so. Try getting there in three or four shots instead. Achieving goals builds confidence.

Chapter 8

MUST-KNOW RULES AND ETIQUETTE

Many of the points covered in this chapter are also discussed elsewhere in the book. But if you read only one chapter, make it this one so that you have the confidence to play golf socially or for business. You may worry about what other golfers think of your swing, but it's how you handle yourself on the course that will stick in their minds. Whether it's a casual round with friends, a member-guest tournament at a private country club, or a business outing with clients, the little things—common courtesies, knowing the rules—mean a lot.

"**Y**ou don't have to be a great player to be great to play with."

—Shelly Rule, LPGA professional and cofounder of Sell thru Golf

RULES SCHOOL

What do you do if you lose your ball? How do you count a whiff? Golf, like any game, has its rules. And we're talking *rules*—34 of them, to be exact. The "Rules of Golf," as they are universally known, are set forth by golf's governing body, the United States Golf Association (USGA) and published as a pint-sized paperback. Any self-respecting golfer should have a copy in her golf bag (see chapter 10, Resources, for how to obtain one). With all due respect to the USGA, the rules are written in inscrutable prose. And frankly, beginners need know only a handful to get going.

• •

"**F**or a quick and simple overview of
etiquette and rules, read the first
dozen or so pages of *The Rules of Golf*,
with definitions of hazards, loose
impediments, and other rules lingo, as
well as key points of etiquette."

—Krista Dunton

• •

So here is an abbreviated version of the key
must-know rules, written as questions or situations that might come up while you're playing. And please, if you aspire to play compet-
itively, get a rules book.

Before we start, it's important to know
that a rules violation will cost you a *penalty
stroke*, maybe even two or more! For example, if you have hit five shots on a hole and
incur a penalty stroke, your score becomes
six. That's bad. In golf you want the lowest
score possible.

Rules to play by

Note that there are different playing formats—stroke play and match play (outlined in chapter
9)—and the penalties sometimes differ. The penalties indicated here are for stroke play, which is
what golfers play most frequently.

How many clubs can I carry? You may carry no more than fourteen clubs during a round
of golf, so count them. If you're caught with more, it'll cost you two or four strokes, depending on
when in the round the infraction is discovered. On discovery of this misdemeanor, take the
offending club or clubs out of the bag and play on.

Where do I tee up the ball? I see a lot of players tee up their ball in front of the tee markers: this is a big no-no. You must tee up the ball between the two markers and not more than two
club lengths behind them. Never, ever tee up in front of the markers. Even in a casual round
where rules may be applied loosely, it's good form to follow this protocol.

Do whiffs count as a stroke? If you swing at the ball and miss, that's a whiff, and it counts
as one stroke. This is possibly one of the most embarrassing, yet hilarious, "shots" in golf.
Everyone, including tour pros Tiger Woods and Nancy Lopez, has whiffed in public. Laugh it off
and carry on with aplomb.

I've lost my ball—now what? Golf courses, with their tree-lined fairways and deep rough,
have voracious appetites for golf balls. Be prepared to lose your fair share of them and know how
to proceed when you do. The Rules of Golf allow you five minutes to search for a lost ball. In a
casual round spend a minute or two, tops. If you don't find your ball, return to the spot from which
you hit your last shot, play another ball, and add one penalty stroke. In golfspeak this is known
as a *stroke-and-distance penalty*. (If you're not competing, keep play moving by dropping a ball near
where you think your original ball was lost, take your one penalty stroke, and play on.)

My ball is out-of-bounds. Those white stakes and fences that border some fairways denote
territory that's out-of-bounds. You'll often find them on courses that are lined with houses (the
owners don't want you foraging for balls in their backyards). If your ball lies outside the stakes (or

anywhere outside the imaginary line between them), it's deemed out-of-play. You must return to the position from which you last hit, play another ball, and add one penalty stroke.

Should I play a provisional ball? Courteous golfers will invoke this rule—it's a huge time-saver. If you fear the ball you just hit landed out-of-bounds or may be lost, declare to your playing partners that you're going to hit a provisional ball—another ball from the same spot you just played from. After you hit the provisional (second) ball, go to where you think your first ball is. If you find it or see that it's not out-of-bounds after all, you must play the original ball. If you don't find the first ball, play the provisional from where it lies, but don't forget to add the one-stroke penalty. On the tee, play the provisional after all others in your group have played. Note: you may not play a provisional for a ball that has gone into a water hazard.

My lie is unplayable. This is a beginner-friendly rule. Golf balls land in the most interesting places—snuggled up to prickly cacti and trees, wedged into the face of a deep bunker, or smack dab in the middle of a

Grounding your club in a bunker or other hazard before you hit your shot is a two-stroke penalty.

patch of poison ivy. Do your score a favor: declare your ball unplayable—it will cost you one penalty stroke—and drop the ball within two club lengths of where it originally lay but no closer to the hole (a ball cannot be deemed unplayable if it's in a water hazard). You'll save yourself the agony—and numerous swings—of trying to hack your way out of a trouble spot. You can also choose to drop a ball behind the point where it lay unplayable, keeping that point directly between the hole and the spot where the ball is dropped, with no limit to how far behind that point the ball may be dropped. Or you can play from where the original ball was last played.

I'm in a sand bunker. If your ball lands in a sand bunker, known as a *hazard*, or other parts of the course also defined as a hazard (water, for example), make sure your club does not touch the sand, the surface of the water, or any ground within the hazard before you hit the ball, including in your backswing. If it does, fess up and tack on two strokes. Ouch.

What are those red and yellow stakes? I still get confused about the difference between red and yellow stakes. Both mark hazards, typically a ditch, stream, pond, or lake. Red stakes indicate a *lateral hazard*—these usually run alongside the fairway—hence *lateral*. You can play from within the hazard (don't ground your club). If that's impossible, under penalty of one stroke, drop the ball outside the hazard on the line on which it first crossed the hazard but no closer to the hole. Yellow stakes usually mark water hazards that are directly in front of where you want to go,

DROPPING THE BALL

In several of the rules situations noted here, you will need to drop your ball, most often one or two club lengths from where it lay, as stipulated by the rules. First mark where the ball lay with a tee. Then pick up your ball and drop it. The proper form for dropping the ball is this: stand erect, hold the ball at arm's length out to your side at shoulder height, and let it fall. You must redrop your ball, without penalty, in these situations:

- It rolls into a hazard, closer to the hole, out-of-bounds, or more than two club lengths from where the ball initially hit when you dropped it.
- You are dropping from a hazard and it rolls out of the hazard.

There are a few other situations when you must redrop, but these are the most common scenarios.

> "I fear failure but overcome this by maintaining a positive mental attitude and by never giving up. One thing that has helped my game is to acquire knowledge, not necessarily physical skill, but playing strategy, course management, rules, etiquette."
>
> —Karen Moraghan, owner, Hunter Public Relations, 25+ handicap

often the green. In the photo below of Heidi Bianchi, a fellow golf nut, dropping the ball (see sidebar), those are yellow stakes. If you hit the ball into the water, drop another one two club lengths from where the ball entered the hazard unless there's a specified drop area.

My ball's on a cart path. If the cart path, a sprinkler head, a drain, or any other immovable man-made obstruction interferes with your stance or swing, you may take "relief"—a free drop from the nearest *point of relief* (basically one club length from the offending object) but no closer to the hole. If the dropped ball lands closer to the hole, you must redrop it. (See Dropping the Ball sidebar.)

ETIQUETTE: THE UNWRITTEN RULES

My husband and I recently played with a couple who are relatively new to the game. Katie was candid about her beginner status—it was her first eighteen-hole round—and assured us she would keep up with the pace of play. And keep up she did. She literally sprinted to her ball between shots. Yet despite this gallant effort, she talked freely when others were teeing off, never tended the pin, and putted out of order.

The proper way to drop a ball.

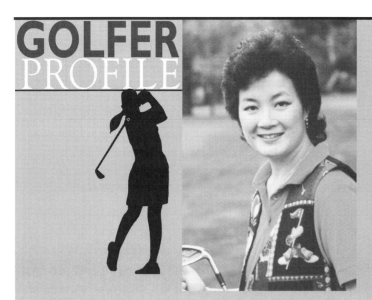

GOLFER PROFILE

SUZANNE WOO

Started golfing: 1987.
Age: 38
Handicap index: 12.8

Suzanne Woo is a real-estate attorney who now runs a business golf consultancy, BizGolf Dynamics, in Berkeley, California. Through her presentations and seminars for individuals and corporate clients, Woo teaches skills to new players, particularly women, to help them develop the confidence to go out on the course with clients. She also offers audiotapes and a booklet with 72 tips for playing business golf. She is writing a book, *Confidence for the Course* (forthcoming 2002). Here's what she has to say.

BUILDING CONFIDENCE FOR THE COURSE

Imagine you want to take a trip to a country you've never visited. If you're like most of us, you'd like to have some knowledge of the place, such as the sights of interest, some native phrases, its traditions and customs. Arriving at a golf course for the first time is similar to landing in a foreign country. It's easy to feel intimidated. Knowing what you'll find at a course—the customs, language, rules, and etiquette—helps you enjoy the game as a full participant rather than a temporary, disengaged visitor.

PLAYING GOLF WITH CLIENTS

If you aren't playing as well as you know you can, don't let it affect your mood and interaction with your playing partners. It's not your score that's important, but rather developing your business relationships.

PLAYING AS A BEGINNER

Play in scramble events if you're a beginner. You don't have to worry about your individual score. Practice your short game and putting before the event. You can contribute to your team's success by chipping and pitching well and sinking long putts.

Contact information for BizGolf Dynamics is in chapter 10, Resources.

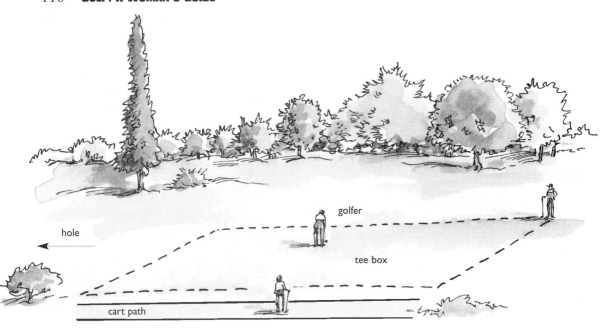

hole

golfer

tee box

cart path

Knowing where to stand while others are hitting their tee shots is a sign of good etiquette.

TIPS FOR PLAYING WITH MEN

• • • • • • • • • • • • • • • • •

"I often play golf with men, but I play from the forward tees. Who should tee off first?"

In mixed company, the golfers playing from the middle or back tees, which come before the forward tees, should hit first, since it helps speed up play. If the tees are just a few yards apart, however, whoever is ready or has the honors should go. If you're in a cart and playing from the forward tees, it's helpful to park in front of the other carts at the tee box so you can go to your tee immediately after the others hit their shots. Unless you're in a tournament, safety and speed of play should come before protocol.

Though there are many nuances in golf, which you will pick up as you play, bone up on these major points of etiquette and you'll be able to play with the best of them. This section is for Katie.

Where to stand. Stand clear of the person hitting and out of her peripheral vision. If possible, avoid standing directly behind a player about to hit, and never stand in the line of fire. On the tee box, stay even with or slightly behind the tee markers. On the putting green, make sure your shadow doesn't fall across a player's line (the imaginary line between the ball and the hole), and don't step on this line.

Talking. Golf is social, and there are plenty of moments between shots to talk and joke around. Never talk on the tee, on the green, or anytime you're within earshot of someone who's swinging the club. Don't jingle your change, rummage through your golf bag, or make any kind of distracting noise, either. And please, no cell phones on the golf course.

Order of play. Flip a coin to determine who has the "honors" on the first hole—golf talk for who goes first. Most people are less formal, and an order is reached by consensus—whoever's

PUTTING PROTOCOL

Your ball is on the green just waiting for you to sink it. But so are three other players' balls. Here's how to proceed.

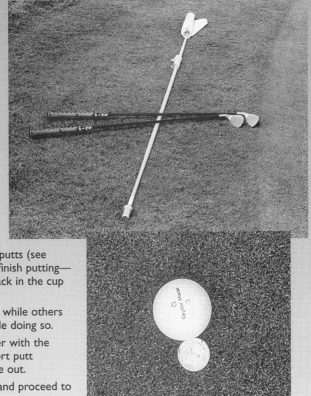

1. Leave your bag and cart behind or to the side of the green in the direction of the next tee (never on the green itself).
2. Repair your ball mark (and others' too; see pages 119, 120).
3. Mark your ball position (see bottom photo). Avoid stepping on other players' lines (the imaginary line between the ball and the hole) as you do so.
4. The player whose ball is closest to the hole tends the pin or pulls it out and lays it down gently off to the side of the green out of the way of all putts (see photo above right). The first player to finish putting—to *hole out*—should put the flagstick back in the cup after everyone has finished.
5. In order to speed play, study your putt while others are hitting, but don't move around while doing so.
6. When it's your turn, replace the marker with the ball, step up, and putt. If you have a short putt remaining, continue putting till you hole out.
7. Clear the green as quickly as possible and proceed to the next hole, where you should mark your scorecard.

Top: Lay extra clubs on the flagstick on the fringe of the putting green so you don't forget them as you exit the green. **Above:** Mark your ball on the putting green by placing a small coin or marker directly behind your ball (the ball is between you and the hole).

• •

"**A**s a beginner, I most feared looking like an idiot. Our performance can be so affected by our nerves, and I was definitely nervous, especially playing around coworkers. The first time I played with my boss I was nervous, but it was so windy, rainy, and cold that we all pretty much played like dogs, and I realized that no one really cares how I play as long as I keep up and have a good time."

—Tara Gravel, associate editor, *Golf Magazine*

• •

ready goes. If you're playing from the forward tees and your partners are playing from the middle or back tees, tee off after they do. It speeds up play.

After the first hole, the person with the lowest score on the previous hole has the honors on the next tee. If it's a tie, the person with the honors from the previous hole carries on. In the fairway or on the green (essentially anywhere else on the course but the tee box) the rules stipulate that the golfer who is *away*, that is, farthest from the hole, should play first. In the interest of faster play, many golfers agree to play *ready golf*, and in informal rounds I heartily recommend it. This simply means you don't stand on ceremony. The golfer who's ready goes first, even if he or she is not away and doesn't have the honors. Always make sure there's no one directly in front of you. It's good to play fast, but you must play safely too.

Be ready to hit when it's your turn. Whether you're playing ready golf or honors, be prepared to go. This means being at your ball with the right club in your hand and knowing what shot you're going to hit.

Keep pace with the group in front of you. Far too many golfers, particularly women, worry about the group behind them. I'm guilty of this, and I can tell you it only adds pressure to your game and adversely affects your performance. It's your duty to keep up with the group of players ahead of you. Be prepared to play as soon as the group is safely out of your range. For example, there may be three foursomes on a golf hole at the same time: a group on the tee, one halfway down the fairway, and one on the green. The group on the green is half a hole ahead of the one on the fairway. That's good. You know you've fallen behind when there's no one ahead of you. For tips on how to speed up play, see chapter 6, Your First Time.

Allow faster golfers to play through. If you're holding up the group behind you it's customary to let the faster group play through. New golfers who habitually take more strokes would be better to just pick up after six or seven shots (or double par) and move ahead rather than to keep letting groups play through. To let players through, step to the sides of the fairway and wave them on. Once they hit their shots and are safely out of your range, continue playing.

Be a good playing partner. Commend good shots (but only once the ball has landed), and don't curse or bemoan your play. Help your partner spot balls so you can locate them quickly. Carry this courtesy throughout the round on all shots. Balls are easily lost in leaves and in the rough.

Know when to pick up your ball. Set a limit per hole—say seven strokes or double par—

after which you will pick up your ball and either put it in your pocket till the next hole or move it to where the other players in your foursome are hitting from. This will speed up play—and reduce your frustration level.

Take only one practice swing. This happens to be my pet peeve. I've seen golfers take five or more practice swings. Take note: this is extremely irritating to other players because it slows down play. And trust me, it won't make you hit the ball any better. Learn to step up to the ball, take one practice swing, then hit.

COURSE MAINTENANCE

Golf courses need your help. Repairing your ball marks (on the greens) and replacing divots (on the fairways) helps the course heal quickly. To be considerate of those playing behind you and to ensure that the course maintenance people have a fair shot at keeping up with the natural wear and tear on the course, leave the course in the same condition you found it in, or better.

Replace or repair divots in the fairway and on the tee box. A divot is a piece of turf you dislodge when you take a full swing (avoid taking divots with your practice swing). If you are playing in

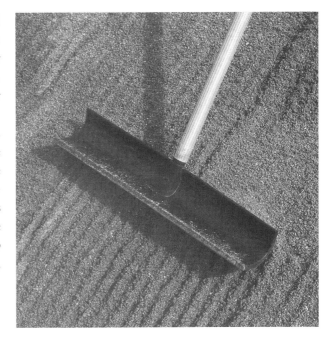

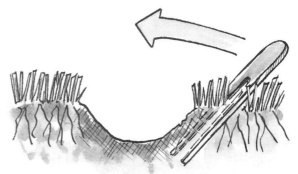

Top: To speed play, rake over your footprints as you exit the bunker.
Above: To repair a ball mark on a green, insert a ball-mark repair tool or a tee at the edge of the mark at a 45-degree angle and bring the edges together with a gentle forward motion. Repeat process, working around the edges of the mark. Gently tamp the surface with your putter.

the South, where Bermuda grass fairways are prevalent, fill in the divot hole with a little sand and grass seed mixture (usually carried on your cart). Up north, where the fairways are typically bent grass, replace the piece of turf and gently tamp it down. If you're in doubt, ask a course employee what the preferred method is.

Repair ball marks on the green. The ball can leave a small indentation or crater on the green. Left unrepaired, it can cause scabs or kill the grass. You'll need a *ball-mark repair tool* or tee to do this properly.

Rake bunkers to smooth out your footprints. You'll find rakes alongside the bunkers (some courses put them in the golf cart). Take the rake into the bunker so you can easily and efficiently rake the marks as you exit. Always exit the bunker the same way you entered.

BUSINESS LINKS

The golf course is the new meeting room of the business world, and there are scads of business golf training programs to prove it. For the most part these are just gussied-up rules and etiquette courses. However, some will help you plan an outing for large groups, so if you're responsible for planning business outings, check chapter 10, Resources, for companies that provide this service.

Otherwise, to play "business golf" simply learn the basic rules and etiquette outlined above and work on your game so that you can shoot about 100 to 105 for eighteen holes.

- Dress the part. It's okay to forgo golf shoes when playing with friends, but a polished look will make a better impression (see chapter 3 for what to wear).

- If you're the person inviting clients, show up early and make certain all their green fees, range balls, and anything else they might have to pay for is taken care of. Also, have plenty of one- and five-dollar bills for tipping.

- If you're the guest, offer to pay for something—lunch, caddie's tip, refreshments after the round. You might be turned down, but at least make a gracious offer.

- Charm your partner by offering to tend the pin for her or gathering her extra clubs as you both exit the green, and don't offer any advice on her swing unless asked.

As for when to talk business, that's up to you.

Chapter 9

HAVE FUN!

Dr. Seuss just might have been talking about golf when he wrote, "Oh, the places you'll go!" By taking lessons and playing casual rounds with friends, you've already got the ball rolling, but you can eat, sleep, and drink golf if you want to. There's literally a world of opportunity for golfers, from local league play to five-star travel around the globe. You can spend your weekends watching golf on TV or go to tournaments as a spectator. You can volunteer your services at pro tour events or carve out a career in the golf industry. And young women can earn full college scholarships on the merit of their golf swings. This chapter provides a brief overview of some of the opportunities to explore. (Complete contact information for the organizations mentioned is listed in chapter 10, Resources.)

"The defining moment when I felt I became a golfer wasn't until I started playing in a league. I had been playing for many years, mostly in business situations but never in a league. I guess that made it official for me. When the starter got to know my name I felt like I wasn't intruding any-more and finally belonged."

—Kim Steuterman Rogers, freelance writer

Golf is a great game to play with old friends, and it also affords the chance to make new ones.

FINDING PLAYING PARTNERS

It's a mistake to dismiss the game because you're afraid you won't have anyone to play with. There are lots of leagues and associations you can join where there are playing partners galore. Here are some helpful hints on where to start looking.

Join the Executive Women's Golf Association or other interest group

Without a doubt the EWGA is the organization to join if you don't belong to a club or have regular playing partners. With 14,000 members spread over ninety-five national chapters and growing, it's the largest membership organization of women golfers. You don't have to be on the corporate fast track to belong or to benefit from membership. The women I've met from three different chapters in the New York area have included stay-at-home moms, teachers, and tax lawyers.

Although the quantity and quality of the chapters' activities can vary widely, they are suitable for anyone from absolute beginners to accomplished players. New golfers can benefit from the golf clinics and seminars on rules and etiquette. There's also a mentor program where the more experienced golfers take new players to the course. And there are plenty of opportunities to get out and play. There are also sectional and national competitions among the chapters. This program is a great way to meet other women golfers, and if you travel to a city or an area that has a chapter, you can get in touch with EWGA members to play some golf or participate in an upcoming event. If there's no chapter in your area, you can even apply to form your own.

Special interests groups have formed national chapters, among them the American Singles Golf Association (you really do have to be unmarried to join), the Blind Golf Association, and the National Amputee Golf Association.

Join a local golf league

It's tough to find a public course that doesn't offer some kind of organized play. It could be Sunday morning couples' golf or a summer evening women's league (evening play continues until dark). Many public courses have membership programs as well, with full-time active leagues and tournaments.

Join a private club

You'll never lack playing partners if you join a private club. I've never been to one that doesn't have a bulletin board in the women's locker room with a full golf calendar and nine-hole and eighteen-hole leagues. One warning: if you want to participate in the events, you'll have to establish a handicap index, a service all private clubs provide (see chapter 4).

The downside, of course, is the cost, which at one extreme can be as high as $300,000 for an initial membership plus monthly dues. But you can also join a club for a few thousand dollars, depending on where you live. Some are by invitation only, and there are waiting lists of five years or more at some prestigious older clubs.

There's no denying that there are still private country clubs (mostly in the Northeast and the South) that restrict women from becoming members or prohibit them from teeing off on Saturday mornings. Happily, however, most new private courses today are part of residential or real estate developments and offer equal access to men and women.

Show up as a single

One of the beauties—and personal challenges—of golf is that you can play as a *single*, which means you show up at a course by yourself with your clubs but without prearranged partners. This is a good tactic to get onto a busy course, and you'll most likely be paired with a twosome or threesome—often men. If you play the same course regularly, you'll become acquainted with course regulars and which groups you fit into readily in terms of temperament and ability.

The prospect of golfing with strangers is daunting for many women—including me. It doesn't matter if they've just taken up the game or have been playing for years; most women just don't like to play golf with people they don't know. But I have to say

"I often go out as a single golfer. That's the beauty of golf, the fact that you don't have to have anybody to play with. You meet a lot of interesting and different people that way, and it's generally a friendly experience."

—Amanda Livingston, two-year golfer

HELP! I'VE BEEN INVITED TO PLAY AT A PRIVATE CLUB

OK, don't panic. Learn this easy country club code and you'll be fine:

- **Dress.** Err on the side of the conservative by wearing a collared shirt and sleek pants or shorts that fall no more than an inch above the knee. Wear a belt and golf shoes. You'll probably be invited to stay for lunch, so bring an appropriate change of clothes. And never change into your golf shoes in the parking lot. Use the locker room for that.

- **Who pays?** The host should pick up the tab, but always offer to reimburse her for the green fee. If your host declines (and with luck she will), ask if you can take care of any caddie fees and tips for yourself and the member.

"**I** golf as a single often. We have joined a semiprivate club in our rural area, and I have never encountered a problem as a woman golfing by myself. At first it was intimidating, but it gets easier. You just have to do it and get used to how it feels. If you follow golf etiquette and are generally courteous to others, people will respect you.

"I've been playing for about four years, so I'm still learning a lot. I still feel like a beginner. Right now my handicap is a 14, but I want to improve and feel it is possible. I am naturally shy, so tournaments make me uncomfortable. We started playing in some this year though, and it's getting easier. All I can say is I love the game and want to play forever. I guess I'm a junkie. The handicap sheet says I turned in 110 rounds this year, if that's any indication of how addicted I am."

—Michelle Morgan, golf nut

From the professional level to local amateur events, there are plenty of opportunities for the competitive woman golfer. Shown here is LPGA Tour pro Dottie Pepper after her victory in the 1999 Nabisco Championship.

that the overwhelming majority of women who do go it alone love the experience. You can meet some wonderful people. When we ran a question in *Golf For Women* asking our readers about their experience playing as singles, the rave responses inspired me to try it. One woman was hooked up with the musician Alice Cooper, an avid golfer, who gave her a Callaway driver at the end of the round!

COMPETING

If you're looking to step up the competitive pressure (not the office scramble) and are a strong bogey golfer or better, consider joining your state or regional golf association. Many have separate women's chapters (to compete at any level, you'll need to establish a handicap index).

These associations are all about playing golf, and their rosters are full of events. Some are quite serious and attract top amateurs who go on to play in USGA events. Some have strict requirements for joining—for example, the New York area's Women's Metropolitan

Golf Association, which was founded more than a century ago, has a handicap index requirement of 18, and members must belong to a private club. But there are many groups that accept individual members with no handicap requirements.

Most associations have Web sites and are easy to find through a quick Internet search. The names are straightforward: for example, the Arizona Women's Golf Association. But first check out the USGA's Web site (www.usga.org) as well as the National Golf Foundation (www.ngf.org), which have association listings, and look at their contact information.

If you're a very good golfer, you may qualify to compete in some of the prestigious amateur events that the USGA stages. Two to aspire to are the U.S. Women's Amateur Public Links and the U.S. Women's Mid-Amateur.

You can also find events ranging from the National Club Championship for Women, which draws female club champions from around the country, to slightly less intense competitions such as the Women's Oldsmobile Scramble, a national team play event open to all amateur golfers.

TRAVEL

You'd be surprised at the number of countries where you can take a fabulous golf vacation, either the plan-it-yourself variety or an all-inclusive one organized by an outfitter, even customized for your foursome. The offerings are amazing, from deluxe river cruises in France with wine tastings to safaris in Africa or biking in Ireland.

This women-only golf trip to Ireland provided a wonderful vacation as well as lifelong friendships and golfing buddies.

WHAT'S THE SCORE? GAMES AND PLAYING FORMATS

Most golfers play *stroke play*, where you keep track of every stroke you take during a round. If you're competing, the player with the fewest net strokes at the end of eighteen holes wins. (Net is your score after you apply your course handicap; see chapter 4.)

If you play in any outings or amateur competitions you'll probably encounter several different games and playing formats. Here's a quick take on some of the more common ones. Scrambles, for example, offer less pressure for new golfers because there are no individual scores to keep track of.

Match Play

Unlike stroke play, *match play* is a hole-by-hole competition. Two players (opponents) compete on each hole rather than comparing their total strokes at the end of the round. Simply put, the player with the lower score on each hole wins that hole, which is worth one point. Some matches go all the way to eighteen holes, but others may end as soon as one person has won more holes than there are left to play. A lot of club events are match play. The beauty is that you could shoot a very high number on one hole and the worst that would happen is you'd lose that hole, since strokes are not carried over. You start fresh on each hole. Handicaps do apply in match play. (See scorecard at right for how to record a match.)

Nassau

A *Nassau* is a simple betting game that adds excitement to a round. An eighteen-hole round is divided into three separate bets: the front nine, the back nine, and the entire eighteen holes. Each bet is worth one point. The winner of each bet is the one who wins the most holes, or who has the lowest score, as in stroke play, on the three separate bets.

Scramble

A *scramble* is a fun format that takes the pressure off individual performance and is often used in group or corporate outings. In a scramble, your foursome becomes a team. Each member of the team hits a tee shot, and the best drive of the four is selected. All players then play their second shots within a foot of that position (you literally pick up your ball and place it close to the selected ball) and so on until the ball is in the cup. In short, play is always from wherever the best shot landed, and the team records one score for the hole.

Bestball

Like a scramble, *bestball* is a team event; the best individual score of the team of players (a foursome or twosome) on any given hole is used as the team score for that hole. Bestball can be played in match play or stroke play formats. Again, it's great for new golfers because it minimizes the pressure to perform.

Hole	Recommended Tees Men/Women	1	2	3	4	5	6	7	8	9	OUT		10	11	12	13	14	15	16	17	18	IN	TOT	HCP	NET
Stone	Permission Only	426	435	227	383	546	194	573	462	448	3694	P	436	163	412	557	200	360	467	427	563	3585	7279		
Black	0-6	399	412	208	354	532	180	542	437	430	3494	L	406	148	373	531	179	334	441	409	540	3361	6855		
Blue	7-15 / 0-4	381	393	181	343	519	157	529	416	407	3326	A	375	137	349	521	154	311	416	390	527	3180	6506		
White	16-26 / 5-14	371	353	167	309	497	147	508	389	329	3070	Y	356	123	315	484	133	302	384	324	496	2917	5987		
Green	27+ / 15+	342	328	146	257	434	125	449	373	257	2711	E	307	96	265	436	118	220	310	283	373	2408	5119		
Grace		5	5	4	5	6	3	5	6	5	44	G	5	5	5	5	4	5	5	6	7	47	91	20	
Molly		6	(5)	4	7	6	4	5	(6)	(6)	49	M	6	4	(5)	8	3	6	(6)	5	6	49	98	25	
Match		+	–	0	+	0	+	0	–	0			+	–	–	+	–	+	0	–	–		–1		
PAR		4	4	3	4	5	3	5	4	4	36		4	3	4	5	3	4	4	4	5	36	72		
HANDICAP		7	(3)	9	17	13	15	11	(5)	(1)			8	18	(4)	14	12	16	(2)	6	10				
DATE				SCORER										ATTESTED BY								TEES				

Match play is hole-by-hole competition (match score is noted from Grace's point of view). Check the scorecard to see on which holes the player with the higher handicap—Molly—gets strokes. She'll get five strokes (the difference in Molly's and Grace's handicaps) on the five lowest-numbered holes as indicated on the scorecard's Handicap row at the bottom of the card; the holes where Molly gets strokes are circled (use a dot or slash if you prefer). On hole 1, Grace's 5 beats Molly's 6, so Grace marks a "+," indicating she won that hole. On hole 2, Molly's 5, or net 4 (she gets a stroke from Grace on this hole, as noted by the circle on the Handicap row at the bottom of the card) beats Grace's 5, so Grace loses that hole, as indicated by the "–" sign. The two tie the third hole, as indicated by the "0." At the end of 18 holes, Grace simply counts the holes she won, 6, and subtracts from that figure the number of holes she lost, 7, to determine that she lost the match by one hole, or –1 in golfspeak.

KEY

+ = player won the hole

– = player lost the hole

O = players tied the hole

How good do you have to be to go on an organized group trip? In Europe you often must have proof of your handicap; requirements can range from 24 to 36 for women. Renting clubs is not a problem at resorts and nice public courses. Even in the north of Portugal, my husband and I played at a lovely course with rental clubs. If you don't want to lug your own clubs, be sure to call and reserve a set before you go.

CAREERS

It's possible to turn your passion for golf into a profession. I consider myself fortunate that I've been able to combine my interest in golf with my career in magazine publishing, which I have pursued for fifteen years.

There are many examples of women who have carved out their own career paths. Suzanne Woo was a corporate lawyer in a previous life before she founded BizGolf Dynamics, a consulting firm that helps bring new golfers up to speed on the rules and etiquette of business golf. And Cathy MacPherson, a former musician who started playing golf at 26, is now an LPGA teaching professional. You can become a golf course superintendent, a pro shop merchandiser, a club manager, a tournament director, a golf course architect—almost any professional skill can be used in the golf industry.

• •

"**B**eing involved in public relations and golf travel writing, specializing in international destinations, has enabled me and my golf clubs to travel the globe professionally and enrich my life personally through all the wonderful people I meet on every trip. Golf is truly an international language spoken and a passion shared in all corners of the world. Even when I'm at the local grocery store, a distinctive logo on a fellow shopper's shirt can trigger a conversation on places played and new 'must-play' experiences that can blossom into a friendship or a new golf partner. I know of no other sport that can take one to so many places— mountains, deserts, fields, beaches, islands, in almost every country—to experience the landscape and the people as intimately as the game of golf. And the best part is, as golf is also a lifelong participatory sport, I'm looking forward to playing and traveling well into my twilight years!"

—Dove Jones, president, Golf Ink

• •

"I started playing golf at 9 and began competing in junior golf tournaments at 10, in between playing soccer and Little League. I wasn't as skilled as the other kids who played full time, but growing up with three brothers, I was a good athlete and very competitive. Basically I would count how many girls were signed up (usually around four or five), then count how many trophies there were. If my chances to win a trophy were good, I was ready to play!

"All the girls I played junior golf with in northern California ended up playing in college and professionally. I played the Futures Tour for four years after college, from 1989 to 1993."

—Krista Dunton, LPGA and PGA teaching professional

If you're more altruistic, you can volunteer at professional tournaments, where armies of helpers are needed to help run things smoothly. You might not get assigned the glamorous posts where you meet the players, but at least you'll be surrounded by golf nuts. If you know an event is coming to town, call the tournament office at the club where it's being held and tell them you're interested in helping out. To find out the schedules of the various professional tours, call the tour headquarters or check their Web sites.

HIGHER EDUCATION

Did you know that dozens of college golf scholarships for young women go unclaimed every year? Check out the *Ping American College Golf Guide*, a publication that lists scholarship opportunities for girls and boys.

Most anywhere you travel, you'll find a golf course.

Published annually in September, this lists every college and university in the United States that has a golf program. It costs about $15, and you can buy it directly from the publisher (see chapter 10, Resources). The guide is distributed free to all members of the American Junior Golf Association. Asterisks alongside coaches' names indicate that scholarship money is available.

🏌 RESOURCES

GENERAL

Golf Channel
7580 Commerce Center Dr.
Orlando FL 32819
407-345-4653
www.thegolfchannel.com
Tune in for 24-hour-a-day golf,
including instruction, pro tour
coverage, and player profiles.

IMG Consumer Golf Shows
IMG Center, Suite 100
1360 E. 9th St.
Cleveland OH 44114
877-898-8780
www.imggolfexpo.com
Showcases latest equipment in
several major cities each year.

National Golf Foundation
1150 S. U.S. Hwy. 1, Suite 401
Jupiter FL 33477
800-733-6006; 561-744-6006
www.ngf.org
Group aimed to promote the game
of golf; publishes golf reports and
books. Membership organization
but lots of good information
available to nonmembers on the
Web site, including golf statistics.

National Minority Golf Foundation
7226 N. 16th St.
Phoenix AZ 85020
602-943-8399
www.nmgf.org
Resource for golf-related programs,
projects, scholarships, and jobs for
minorities.

Professional Golf Association
   of America
100 Ave. of Champions
Palm Beach Gardens FL 33410
561-624-8400
www.pga.com
Not to be confused with the PGA
Tour, this organization is a good
source of information on finding
teaching pros.

United States Golf Association
   (USGA)
P.O. Box 746
Far Hills NJ 07931
800-223-0041; 908-234-2300
www.usga.org
Contact this membership organization to obtain a copy of *The Rules
of Golf,* handicap information, and

listings of state and local golf associations. Its Web site is an excellent source of all of the above.

World Golf Hall of Fame
21 World Golf Place
St. Augustine FL 32092
904-940-4123
www.wgv.com/wgvfhalloffame.
   html

PROFESSIONAL TOURS

An outing to watch the top pros in action is a must for aspiring golfers. Contact for tournament and TV schedules, player profiles and stats.

Futures Golf Tour
1300 Eaglebrooke Blvd.
Lakeland FL 33813
863-709-9100
www.futurestour.com
The developmental tour for the LPGA.

Ladies Professional Golf
   Association (LPGA)
100 International Golf Dr.
Daytona Beach FL 32124
904-274-6200
www.lpga.com
The LPGA Web site also has information on where to find teaching professionals in your area, an on-line pro shop, junior golf programs, and more.

Professional Golfers' Association
   (PGA Tour)
112 PGA Tour Blvd.
Ponte Vedra Beach FL 32082
904-285-3700
www.pgatour.com
PGA tour events are where to see Tiger Woods in action.

FOR JUNIOR GOLFERS

American Junior Golf Association
   (AJGA)
1980 Sports Club Dr.
Braselton GA 30517
877-373-2542; 770-868-4200
www.ajga.org

International Junior Golf Tour
   (IJGT)
P.O. Box 5130
Hilton Head Island SC 29938
843-785-2444
www.ijgt.com

LPGA Girls Golf Club
100 International Golf Dr.
Daytona Beach FL 32124
904-274-6200
www.lpga.com
Introductory golf programs (instruction, on-course playing) for girls 7 to 17 at 70+ sites across the country.

National Association of Junior
   Golfers (NAJA)
11891 U.S. Hwy. 1, Suite 101
North Palm Beach FL 33408
561-691-3871
www.najg.org

National Golf Coaches
   Association (NGCA)
500 N. Michigan Ave.,
   Suite 1530
Chicago IL 60611
312-670-7840
www.ngca.com
Organizes Get a Girl Golfing, a nationwide initiative to introduce girls to the sport.

Ping
See contact information under

Manufacturers of Women's Equipment Lines; see also *The Ping American College Golf Guide*, under books.

MAGAZINES

Golf & Travel
P.O. Box 420235
Palm Coast FL 32142
800-678-9717
www.travelgolf.com/golfandtravel/

Golf Digest
P.O. Box 3125
Harlan IA 51593
800-PAR-GOLF (800-727-4653)
www.golfdigest.com
Publishes a quarterly women's supplement.

Golf For Women
P.O. Box 37465
Boone IA 50037
800-374-7941
www.golfforwomen.com
The only stand-alone women's golf magazine. Instruction, equipment reviews, fitness. Publishes annual guides to the best courses, teaching professionals, and golf shops for women.

Golf Magazine
P.O. Box 53733
Boulder CO 80322
800-876-7726
www.golfonline.com
Geared toward a male audience but good travel information.

T&L Golf
1901 Bell Ave.
Des Moines IA 50315
800-947-7961
www.travelandleisuregolf.com

BOOKS

Alfredsson, Helen, and Amy Ellis Nutt. *A Good Swing Is Hard to Find: How Women Can Play the Power Game*. New York: Doubleday, 1998.

Ladies Professional Golf Association. *LPGA's Guide to Every Shot*. Champaign IL: Human Kinetics, 2000.

Leonard, Terri, ed. *In the Women's Clubhouse: The Greatest Women Golfers in Their Own Words*. Lincolnwood IL: Contemporary, 2000.

Mallon, Bill. *The Golf Doctor: How to Play a Healthier, Better Round of Golf*. New York: Macmillan, 1996.

Owens, DeDe, and Dan Kirschenbaum. *Smart Golf: How to Simplify and Score Your Mental Game*. San Francisco: Jossey-Bass, 1998.

Penick, Harvey, and Edwin Shrake. *For All Who Love the Game: Lessons and Teachings for Women*. New York: Simon & Schuster, 1995.

Ping American College Golf Guide. 2000–2001 edition. Hillsboro OR: Dean Frischknecht, 2000. This annual publication lists scholarship opportunities for girls and boys. Lists colleges and universities in the U.S. that have a golf program. Asterisks by the coaches' names indicate whether or not there is scholarship money available. You can buy the book for about $15 directly from the publisher or online at www.collegegolf.com. The book is distributed free to members of the AJGA.

Russell, Mark. *Golf Rules Plain and Simple*. New York: HarperResource Book, 1999.

Saunders, Vivien. *The Golf Handbook for Women: The Complete Guide to Improving Your Game*. New York: Three Rivers Press, 2000.

Shoemaker, Fred, and Pete Shoemaker. *Extraordinary Golf: The Art of the Possible*. New York: Putnam's, 1996.

United States Golf Association. *The Rules of Golf 2000–01*. U.S. Golf Association, 800-223-0041; www.usga.org.

Valentine, Linda, and Margie Hubard. *Golf Games within the Game: 200 Fun Ways Players Can Add Variety and Challenge to Their Game*. New York: Perigee, 1992.

Vold, Mona. *Different Strokes: The Lives and Teachings of the Game's Wisest Women*. New York: Simon & Schuster, 1999.

Wolkodoff, Neil. *Physical Golf: The Golfer's Guide to Peak Conditioning and Performance*. Denver: KickPoint Press, 1997.

Wright, Mickey. *Play Golf the Wright Way*. Dallas: Taylor, 1990.

VIDEOS AND TRAINING AIDS

The Golf Coach Inc.
5060 N. Royal Atlanta Dr., Suite 28
Tucker GA 30084
800-772-3813; 770-414-9508
www.golfcoachinc.com
Great selection of training aids.

GolfSmart
P.O. Box 2626
Grass Valley CA 95945
800-637-3557
www.golfsmart.com
Golf books, videos, computer software, training aids.

WEB SITES FOR WOMEN

Web sites come and go so quickly that I'm reluctant to promote them. But these have been around for a while.

Fore Women Golfers
www.womengolfers.com
Publishes a newsletter with tips as well.

GolfClubforWomen.com
www.golfclub4women.com
Offers news, events, tips, tour coverage, online pro shop.

Women on the Green
www.womenonthegreen.com
Offers resources, merchandise.

Women's Golf Today
www.womensgolftoday.com
Offers resources, merchandise.

TRAVEL

Golf & Travel
See contact information under Magazines.

Golf International
14 E. 38th St., 15th Floor
New York NY 10016
800-833-1389
www.golfinternational.com
Specializes in trips to Scotland and Ireland.

InterGolf
P.O. Box 500608
Atlanta GA 31150
800-468-0051
www.intergolfvacations.com
Well-priced golf tours around
the world.

Jerry Quinlan's Celtic Golf
P.O. Box 608
Cape May Court House NJ 08210
800-535-6148
www.jqcelticgolf.com
Specializes in trips to Scotland
and Ireland.

Kalos Golf
104 N. Elliott Rd.
Chapel Hill NC 27514
800-314-3162; 919-929-2990
info@kalosgolf.com
www.kalosgolf.com
Golf cruises with top teaching
pros onboard.

Ridgewater Partners
2091 Stratford Pl.
Santa Barbara CA 93108
805-969-5962
Small outfitter; offers golf cruises
and one women's-only trip.

T&L Golf
See contact information under
Magazines.

Travel.com
www.travel.com
This Web site reviews resorts and
public courses around the country
and beyond.

Wide World of Golf
P.O. Box 5217
Carmel CA 93921

800-214-4653
www.wideworldofgolf.com

GOLF SCHOOLS AND FINDING A PRO

To contact the women professionals quoted in this book, or to find
a qualified teaching professional in
your area, call the LPGA at 904-
274-6200 or go to www.lpga.com
and click on Teaching & Club
Pros for a listing of instructors
by region. Or, call the PGA or go
to www.pga.com and click on
Learning Center, then Pro Central.

Here's a selection of well-
established golf schools that offer
programs for women and new
golfers. Unless otherwise noted,
the programs are open to men and
women. For further help in choosing a school, consult *The Guide to
Golf Schools and Camps* (Shaw
Guides, Inc., P.O. Box 231295,
New York NY 10023, 212-799-
6464, http://golf.shawguides.com/).

Ben Sutton Golf School
P.O. Box 9199
Canton OH 44711
800-225-6923
www.golfschool.com
Schools are held in Florida.

Coaching for the Future with
    Lynn Marriott and Pia Nilsson
Legacy Golf Resort
6808 S. 32nd St.
Phoenix AZ 85040
888-828-FORE (888-828-3673);
    602-305-5550
www.coachingforthefuture.com
Programs for low-handicap
women, juniors, and men.

Craft-Zavichas Golf School
600 Dittmer
Pueblo CO 81005
800-858-9633
www.czgolfschool.com
Women-only programs year-round
in California, Colorado, and
Minnesota.

Dana Rader Golf School
Ballantyne Resort
10000 Ballantyne Commons
    Parkway
Charlotte NC 28277
877-99-RADER (877-997-2337);
    704-542-7635
www.ballantyneresort.com/
    playhome.html

Golf Divas
Crystal Springs Golf Course
6650 Golf Course Dr.
Burlingame CA 94010-6598
650-342-4188, x33

JoAnne Carner Golf Academy
    for Ladies
7500 St. Andrews Rd.
Lake Worth FL 33467
561-965-0044
www.palmbeachnational.com/jcga
Intermediate and advanced
sessions.

Krista Dunton
Forsgate Country Club
Jamesburg NJ 08831
732-656-8909
E-mail: KDswingdoc@aol.com
Private lessons, schools, and
corporate outings.

Marlene Floyd's "For Women
    Only" Golf School
5350 Clubhouse Lane

Hope Mills NC 28348
800-637-2694
www.marlenefloyd.com

Nancy Quarcelino School of Golf
Legends Club of Tennessee
1500 Legends Club Lane
Franklin TN 37069
615-599-1344
www.the-q-school-of-golf.com

Pebble Beach Golf Academy
P.O. Box 658
Pebble Beach CA 93953
831-622-8650
www.pebblebeach.com
Corporate women's schools.

Pine Needles Golfari
1005 Midland Rd.
Southern Pines NC 28388
800-747-7272
www.rossresorts.com/
    golfpineneedlesintro.html
Several women's-only weeks
each year.

Positive Strokes
Melissa Whitmire
P.O. Box 39344
Greensboro NC 27438
336-545-3265
www.happinessingolf.com

Rina Ritson Golf School
8991 Gladin Court
Orlando FL 32819
407-876-0150
www.rinagolf.com

Sandra Haynie Golf Experience
P.O. Box 261730
Highlands Ranch CO 80163
817-291-1868
www.sandrahayniegolf.com

School of Extraordinary Golf
27505 Via Sereno
P.O. Box 22731
Carmel CA 93922
800-541-2444; 831-625-1900
Extragolf@aol.com
Innovative approach, schools,
and couples workshops.

School of Golf for Women
Singing Hills Resort
3007 Dehesa Rd.
El Cajon CA 92019
888-764-4566; 619-442-3425
www.singinghills.com/
    information/index4.html
One of the original women's-only
golf schools.

Women to the Fore
The Boulders
34631 N. Tom Darlington Dr.
Carefree AZ 85377
800-553-1717; 480-488-9009
www.wyndham.com/boulders/
    default.cfm#
Good introductory packages
for women.

BUSINESS GOLF LINKS

Regional and national programs
and consultants who will teach the
nuances of the game (basically rules
and etiquette reviews) to companies
and individuals who need to play
golf for business. Some will help
organize corporate outings as well.

BizGolf Dynamics
2003 Milvia St., Suite B
Berkeley CA 94704
800-722-8909; 510-233-9290
www.bizgolfdynamics.com
Seminars, video, audiotapes,
workbook.

Business Golf Strategies, Inc.
Bill Storer
28 Cross Rd.
Basking Ridge NJ 07920
908-204-9350
www.businessgolfstrategies.com

Business Golf Unlimited
Judy Anderson
42253 Parkside Circle, Suite 105
Sterling Heights MI 48314
810-739-8506
www.bizgolf.com

Business on the Links
1 Marlwood Lane
Palm Beach Gardens FL 33418
561-627-4987
nancy_oliver@businessonthelinks.
    com
www.businessonthelinks.com
Offers a video on playing business
golf.

Golf Matters
Susan Weitzman
1725 Overland Trail
Deerfield IL 60015
847-945-0390
www.golfmattersinc.com

Sell Thru Golf
600 17th St., Suite 950 S.
Denver CO 80202
303-405-8333
www.sellthrugolf.com

GOLF FOR THE DISABLED

For pros who specialize in working
with disabled golfers, or those with
special needs, contact the LPGA
Teaching and Club Professional
Division.

Every Body Golf School
Noel Jablonski
3200 Jermantown Rd.
Oakton VA 22124
703-255-5396
www.everybodygolf.com

Fore All
P.O. Box 2456
Kensington MD 20891
301-881-1818
www.foreall.org
A nonprofit organization designed to help disabled individuals play golf.

National Amputee Golf
  Association
11 Walnut Hill Rd.
Amherst NH 03031
800-633-NAGA (800-633-6242)
www.amputee-golf.org

U.S. Blind Golf Association
c/o Bob Andrews, President
3094 Shamrock St. N.
Tallahassee FL 32308
850-893-4511
www.blindgolf.com/unitedstates/
  ushomepage.htm

United States Golf Association
  (USGA)
See contact information under General (pages 131–32). The USGA has a Resource Center for Individuals with Disabilities, a national clearinghouse of information for those with disabilities seeking to play golf.

COMPETITIONS AND EVENTS FOR WOMEN

Here's a listing of some events for women golfers. For more serious amateur competiton, check out the USGA's tournament schedule.

DuPont CoolMax World Amateur
  Handicap Championship
754 Howard Parkway
Myrtle Beach SC 29577
800-833-8798
www.worldamateur.com
The largest annual amateur golf competition in the world. Open to all with a handicap index. Women's, men's, and team events.

Golf Digest Women's National
  Club Championship
P.O. Box 158989
Nashville TN 37215
615-783-0073
Annual event open to women who have won their club championships.

LPGA Golf Clinics for Women
197 8th St.
Flagship Wharf
Boston MA 02129
800-262-PUTT (800-262-7888)
www.jbcgolf.com
Series of introductory one-day clinics around the country.

Rally for a Cure with *Golf For
  Women* magazine
P.O. Box 579
Ridgefield CT 06877
800-327-6811
www.rallyforacure.com
Year-round national one-day golf events at public and private courses around the country to raise breast cancer awareness. Benefits Susan G. Komen Foundation.

RE/MAX World Long Drive
  Championship, Women's
  Division

Long Drivers of America
395 W. Hwy. 114, Suite 300
Southlake TX 76092
888-233-4654; 909-949-9901
www.longdrivers.com
If you can bomb your tee shots more than 220 yards, consider entering this annual competition, which offers prize money to the top finishers. Regional qualifiers start each year in April and finals are held in October.

Take Your Daughter to the Golf
  Course Week
National Golf Course Owners
  Association
1470 Ben Sawyer Blvd.,
  Suite 18
Mt. Pleasant SC 29464
800-933-4262
www.getlinkedplaygolf.com
Annual event held each spring with the goal of getting parents to introduce their daughters to golf.

Women in Golf Day
See American Golf Corp. contact information under League Play. The free event is geared to introduce women to the game, with clinics on rules and etiquette, driving a cart, and golf instruction. Held annually the first Saturday after Mother's Day at each of the 300+ public, resort, and private courses owned and operated by the American Golf Corporation.

Women's Oldsmobile Scramble
127 Industrial Ave.
Coldwater MI 49036
800-582-1908
www.womensscramble.com

Team event with local qualifiers for the national championship.

LEAGUE PLAY

To locate a women's state or local golf association (most associations offer league play, events, handicap services) in your area, check out these Web sites: the United States Golf Association (www.usga.org), the National Golf Foundation (www.ngf.org), and GolfLink.com (www.golflink.com). Golf Handicap and Information Network (GHIN), the largest handicap service provider, also has listings on its Web site, www.ghin.com.

American Golf Corporation
American Golf Players
    Association
3443 N. Central Ave., Suite 819
Phoenix AZ 85012
888-790-AGPA (888-790-2472)
www.agpa.com
www.americangolf.com
Offers membership programs at its public and private courses.

American Singles Golf Association
P.O. Box 470493
Charlotte NC 28247
888-GOLFMATE (888-465-3628);
    800-599-2815
www.singlesgolf.com
National organization with local chapters.

Executive Women's Golf
    Association (EWGA)
300 Ave. of the Champions,
    Suite 140
Palm Beach Gardens FL 33418
800-407-1477
www.ewga.com

Local chapters for women golfers of all abilities. League play, events, golf clinics. No business experience necessary!

Fairways Club International
2 National Fairways
107 John St.
Southport CT 06490
877-804-6600
www.fairwaysinternational.com
Membership program at private courses around the United States and a few abroad.

EQUIPMENT

Retail and catalog

I've yet to find a national catalog, shop, or Web site that has a comprehensive selection of women's gear, so you'll have to shop around to find what you're looking for. The following resources have limited selections of good quality women's merchandise (clubs, bags, balls, gloves, and other accessories). If you're looking for a specific brand, it's best to contact the maunfacturer first to find out where its products are sold.

Edwin Watts Golf
20 Hill Ave.
Fort Walton Beach FL 32548
800-874-0146
www.edwinwatts.com

Empowered Women's Golf
400 N. Bowman Rd.
Little Rock AR 72211
501-219-1797
www.empoweredwomensgolf-lr.
    com
Small chain of women's-only golf

stores with equipment, bags, shoes, accessories, and apparel.

Golfsmith
11000 N. IH-35
Austin TX 78753
800-815-3873
www.golfsmith.com

iGolfstore
622 W. State St.
Garland TX 75040
800-966-0161
www.ladiesgolfclubs.com
Offers Square Two and Nancy Lopez Golf clubs plus bags, shoes, and other accessories.

Women's Golf Catalog
P.O. Box 222
Arlington VT 05250
800-984-7324
www.womensgolf.com
Catalog and online store.

Women's Pro Shop
426 Penn Ave.
Drexel Hill PA 19026
888-278-2199; 610-626-1427
www.thewomensproshop.com
Apparel, equipment, and accessories. Offers petite and plus sizes.

Manufacturers of women's equipment

Alexa Stirling
2000 Business Center Dr.,
    Suite 250
Savannah GA 31405
800-465-3313
www.cornerstonegolf.com
Clubs.

Avant
880 Wooster Rd. W.
Barberton OH 44203
800-445-1898
www.sutherlandgolf.com
High-performance golf balls for
women.

Callaway Golf
2285 Rutherford Rd.
Carlsbad CA 92008
800-228-2767
www.callawaygolf.com
Clubs, balls, and bags.

Cleveland Golf
5630 Cerritos Ave.
Cypress CA 90630
800-999-6263
www.clevelandgolf.com
Clubs.

Cobra Golf
2819 Loker Ave. E.
Carlsbad CA 92008
800-223-3537
www.cobragolf.com
Clubs, bags, and balls.

La Jolla Club
2445 Cades Way
Vista CA 92083
800-468-7700
www.lajollaclub.com
Clubs (good junior collection, too).

Lange Golf
15866 W. 7th Ave., Suite E
Golden CO 80401
800-442-2321
www.langegolf.com
Custom-fitted clubs.

Nancy Lopez Golf
18 Gloria Lane
Fairfield CT 07004

888-PLAY-NLG (888-752-9654)
www.nancylopezgolf.com
Clubs, bags, balls, gloves, and
accessories.

Ping
2201 W. Desert Cove
Phoenix AZ 85029
800-4-PING-FIT (800-474-6434)
www.pinggolf.com
Clubs and bags.

Square Two Golf
18 Gloria Lane
Fairfield CT 07004
800-526-2250
www.squaretwo.com
Clubs, bags.

TaylorMade Golf
5545 Fermi Court
Carlsbad CA 92008
800-888-2582
www.taylormadegolf.com
Clubs, bags, and balls.

Titleist
1812 Aston Ave.
Carlsbad CA 92008
888-324-4766
www.titleist.com
Clubs, balls, and gloves.

Top Flite/Spalding Sports
425 Meadow St.
Chicopee MA 01021
800-438-4025; 413-536-1200
www.topflite.com
Clubs, balls, bags, and gloves.

Wilson Golf
8700 W. Bryn Mawr Ave.
Chicago IL 60631
800-469-4576
www.wilsonsports.com
Clubs, balls, bags, and gloves

Yonex Golf
3520 Challenger St.
Torrance CA 90503
800-44-YONEX (800-449-6639)
www.yonex.com
Clubs.

Bags

Bloomingbags
722 Genevieve St., Suite A
Solana Beach CA 92075
800-443-2247
www.bloomingbags.com
Also accessories for women.

Burton Golf
654 Anchors St.
Fort Walton Beach FL 32548
800-633-4630
www.burtongolf.com

Izzo Systems
1635 Commons Parkway
Macedon NY 14502
800-284-1220
www.izzo.com
The best double shoulder strap
golf bags.

Sun Mountain
301 N. 1st St.
Missoula MT 59802
800-227-9224
www.sunmountain.com
Bags, outerwear, and carts.

Shoes and apparel

Adidas Golf
5545 Fermi Court
Carlsbad CA 92008
800-456-8633; 760-918-3540
www.adidasgolf.com

Ashworth
2791 Loker Ave. W.

Carlsbad CA 92008
800-627-4274; 760-438-6610
www.ashworthinc.com

Astra
1430 Broadway, 22nd Floor
New York NY 10018
888-566-9696
www.astragolf.com
Apparel.

Bette & Court
860 W. 84th St.
Hialeah FL 33014
800-862-3883
www.bette-court.com

Cutter & Buck
2701 1st Ave., Suite 500
Seattle WA 98121
800-929-9299
www.cutterbuck.com
Has some retail stores.

Elandale
4349 Baldwin Ave.
El Monte CA 91731
800-532-4808
www.elandale.com

E. P. Pro
8 W. 40th St., 2nd Floor
New York NY 10018
800-462-5419
www.eppro.com

Hanasport
22865 Lockness Ave.
Torrance CA 90501
800-938-4262
www.hanasport.net

Izod Club
P.O. Box 510
Lyons GA 30436

800-522-6783
www.izod.com
Clothing.

J. Lindeberg On Course
111 Greene St., 2nd Floor
New York NY 10012
800-804-7884
www.jloc.com
Clothing.

Lizgolf (Liz Claiborne)
1 Claiborne Ave.
North Bergen NJ 07047
800-555-9838
www.lizclaiborne.com
Clothing.

Nike Golf
1 Bowerman Dr.
Beaverton OR 97005
800-344-6453
www.nikegolf.com
Shoes, balls, bags, and apparel.

Resort Two
2100 5th Ave.
Seattle WA 98121
888-362-7800

Scott & Sterling
910 Skokie Blvd., Suite 106
Northbrook IL 60062
800-231-0093
Sizes 2–16; golf shorts and pants
with slimming front panel insert.

Sugar Mag Golf & Sport
227 N. Old Woodward Ave.
Birmingham MI 48009
248-594-9255
www.sugarmagsport.com

Tehama
823 Milford St.

Glendale CA 91203
800-955-9400
www.tehamainc.com

Clothing and accessories with high SPF

GustBuster
1966-B Broadhollow Rd.
Farmingdale NY 11735
888-487-8287
www.gustbuster.com
Sturdy sun and rain umbrellas.

Solar Eclipse
8240 E. Gelding Dr., Suite 102
Scottsdale AZ 85260
800-878-9600
www.solareclipse.com

Sun Precautions
2815 Wetmore Ave.
Everett WA 98201
800-882-7860
www.sunprecautions.com

Just shoes

Bite Golf
P.O. Box 5012
Preston WA 98050
800-248-3465
www.bite-golf.com

Dexter
71 Railroad Ave.
Dexter ME 04930
888-8DEXTER (888-833-9837)
www.dextershoe.com

Etonic
425 Meadow St.
Chicopee MA 01021
800-772-5346
www.etonic.com
Also gloves.

FootJoy
333 Bridge St.
Fairhaven MA 02719
800-225-8500
www.footjoy.com
Socks, gloves, and outerwear as
    well as shoes.

Lady Fairway
3803 Coporex Dr., Suite 400
Tampa FL 33619
800-770-LADY (800-770-5239)
www.ladyfairway.com
Also gloves and socks.

Tags Golf
175 Clearbrook Rd.
Elmsford NY 10523
800-585-TAGS (800-585-8247)
www.tagsgolf.com

FITNESS RESOURCES

Body Balance for Performance
280 E. Magnolia Blvd.
Burbank CA 91502
888-348-4653
www.fitgolf.com
Golf fitness training program.
Call for locations.

Canyon Ranch Health Resort
8600 E. Rockcliff Road
Tucson AZ 85750
800-726-9900
www.canyonranch.com
Golf-specific exercise program and
instruction.

GMP Fitness
P.O. Box 283
Saddle River NJ 07458
888-467-3488; 845-369-9022
www.gmpfitness.com
Fitness products and videos
for golfers.

PGA National Resort and Spa
400 Avenue of the Champions
Palm Beach Gardens FL 33418
800-633-9150; 561-627-2000
www.pga-resorts.com
Golf conditioning programs,
academy, and spa.

Physical Therapy Services of
    Huntington
Alan Klein, MSPT
232 E. Main St.
Huntington NY 11743
631-673-8070
Sports-related injury treatment and
prevention. Special golf program.

Index

Numbers in **bold** refer to pages with illustrations

scramble (game format), 126
scratch golfers, 51
setup
    chipping, **76**
    pitching, 79
    putting, **74**
setup, for swing. *See also* swing
    aiming, 67–**68**
    ball position, 66–67
    grip, **61**, **64**–**65**
    model, **60**, 61
    posture, 65–**66**
shaft, of golf club, **31**, 32, **34**
    flex and length, 34, 38
Shoemaker, Fred, 27–28
shoes, **43**, 87, 110
short game, 72
    chipping, **73**, 75, **76**–78
    pitching, **73**, 75, **77**, **78**–79
    putting, **73**–**75**
    sand shots, 79–80
short grass, 48
short irons, 38
shots, choosing, 79, 101, 109
shoulder position
    setup, 66
    swing, **69**
side stretch, standing, **102**
significant other, playing with, 16. *See also* partners
single, playing as, 123–24
slope, on scorecards, 55
sole, of golf club, **31**, **34**
Sommers, Darlene, 106
special interest groups, 122
speeding play, **89**, 90, 92
spikes, changing, **43**
spotting balls, 90–91, 92
spouses, 15, 16, 27–28
stance
    chip, **76**
    swing, **65**–**66**
stand bag, **41**
starter attendants, 87, 89
starter sets (golf clubs), 31–32
Steinbach, Debbie, 21, 66
Sternberg, Stina, 42
strangers, golfing with, 123–24
stretching exercises, **102**–**5**

stroke, 46
stroke-and-distance penalty, 112
stroke play, 52–**53**, 126
stroke savers, 100–101, 106–10
sun protection, 44
sweet spot, of golf club, **34**
swing. *See also* preshot routine; setup; setup, for swing
    don'ts, 71–**72**
    drills, **82**–84
    practice techniques, 81–82
    rhythm, 70, 74, 109–10
    step by step, 68–**70**, **71**
swing assist trainer, **82**
swing model, **60**–61
swing plane, **70**, **71**
swing speed, 34, 39, 98

T

takeaway, of swing, **60**
target line, 67, **68**, **71**
tee box (teeing ground), 45, **46**, **47**, 50
teeing off, 89, 90–91, 116
"teeing up with trouble," 91, 101
tee it up, 47
tee markers, 48, **90**, 112
tee sets, colors of, 52, 54
tee set selection
    choosing by skill level, 52, 54
    determining course length, 48, 54
    playing in regulation, 51
tees (pegs), 47, **90**, **110**
tee times, 45, 47, 86
tempo, 70, 74, 109–10
ten-finger (baseball) grip, **65**
"that's a gimme," 95
"that's good," 95
Thompson, Annette, 29
time, for ball search, 92
time per hole, 92
toe, of golf club, **31**, **34**
towels, 43
travel bag, 41
travel, golf vacations, **125**, 128
triple bogeys, 51
turn (halfway point), 95

U

unplayable lie, 101, 113
upper body position
    backswing, **69**
    swing setup, 60, **66**
upper body strengthening drill, **82**
USGA (United States Golf Association), 13, 55, 57, 111

V

visualizing, the target, 67–**68**, 101, 108, 109
volunteering for events, 129

W

walk-ons, at golf courses, 86
warm-up stretches, 100, **102**–**5**
water hazards, 49, 114
weather, 43–44, 100
wedges, 38, 67, 80
whiffs, 46, 88, 112
white stakes, 49
Whitmire, Melissa, 14, 15, 17
wind, judging effect of, 100
women, situations unique to
    bustline, 22, 72
    tee selection, 45, 48
    unrated tees, 55
women golfers
    discrimination against, 13
    number of, 11
    stereotyped as slow, 92
women pros, 22
women's equipment, 32–33, 40
Woo, Suzanne, **115**
woods, **36**, 80, 98
wormbusters, 108
wrist flexion and extension stretch, **105**

Y

yardage markers, **99**, 100
yardage signs, for tees sets, 52, **54**
yellow stakes, 49, 113–14